ANGEL
NUMBERS
101

Also by Doreen Virtue

ANGEL
NUMBERS
101

THE MEANING OF 111, 123, 444, AND OTHER NUMBER SEQUENCES

DOREEN VIRTUE

HAY HOUSE, INC.
Carlsbad, California • New York City
London • Sydney • Johannesburg
Vancouver • New Delhi

Published and distributed in the United States by: Hay House, Inc.: www.hayhouse.com • *Published and distributed in Australia by:* Hay House Australia Pty. Ltd.: www.hayhouse.com.au • *Published and distributed in the United Kingdom by:* Hay House UK, Ltd.: www.hayhouse.co.uk • *Published and distributed in the Republic of South Africa by:* Hay House SA (Pty), Ltd.: www.hayhouse.co.za • *Distributed in Canada by:* Raincoast Books: www.raincoast.com • *Published in India by:* Hay House Publishers India: www.hayhouse.co.in

Editorial supervision: Jill Kramer • *Design:* Tricia Breidenthal

Library of Congress Control Number: 2007943517

ISBN: 978-1-4019-2001-2

28 27 26
1st edition, July 2008

Printed in the United States of America

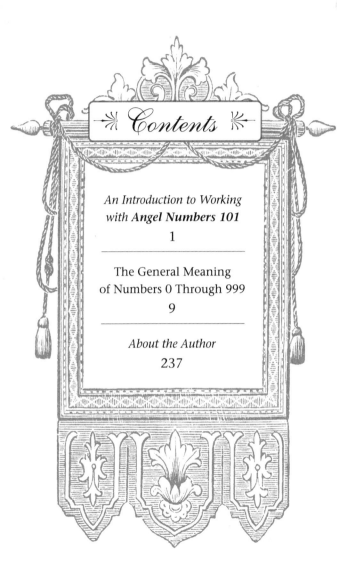

Contents

AN INTRODUCTION
TO WORKING WITH
Angel Numbers 101

When we ask the angels for help, they always answer . . . and sometimes they respond with direct intervention. For instance, you ask for a better job and *voilà!*—a friend telephones to say that her wonderful company is now hiring. Most of the time, though, the angels answer us with Divine guidance.

Divine guidance leads us in positive and healthful directions, and it can come to us as intuitive feelings, brilliant ideas, visions and dreams, or signs. Signs include anything significant we see or hear that answers our questions or needs.

For instance, you wonder if the angels are with you and you look down and see a white feather on your office floor . . . but there's no logical source for the feather. Or you wonder which healing profession you'd most enjoy studying and within one week, three different people bring up the subject of herbology.

One of the most common signs the angels send us are number sequences such as 111, 333, and 1234. Numbers are among the primary tools that angels use to communicate with us. You might see these sequences on automobile license plates, telephone numbers, grocery-store receipts, or the change that a clerk hands to you.

Most people notice the repetition of certain number sequences and begin to wonder, *What does this mean?* I'm among those who are curious about number symbology. As a longtime student of Pyththagorean numerology, I've wondered whether repetitive digits are significant beyond their mathematical functions. My studies show me that they are!

The angels taught me long ago that they'll help us with anything, provided that we ask for that assistance. After all, the angels can't violate our free will. Instead, they wait for us to request help before they're allowed to intervene in our lives.

Over the years, I've discovered that there are no limits as far as the areas in which the angels can assist us (and believe me I've searched!). Our celestial guardians want to help us with every nuance of life including health, happiness, fears, career and finances, relationships, family, travel, and so forth.

So when I wondered about the meaning of number sequences, it was only a matter of time before I had the "aha!" realization that I could ask the angels for help with that, too. So I sat in meditation with paper and pen (and occasionally with my laptop) and went down the list of numbers from 0 through 999. The angels gave me keys to understanding the vibrational meanings of each number, and the cumulative significance of *groups* of numbers.

I first published my findings in a section of my book *Healing with the Angels*. That one chapter generated a strong reaction from my readers and workshop attendees, who wanted to know the meaning behind their particular number sequences. So I put together a little pocket book called *Angel Numbers* to address their questions. In the meantime, I continued asking the angels for information about the meanings of numbers. The additional information they gave me warranted an entirely new book.

The more that I give "angel number readings," the more I find the exquisite simplicity in this message system. In fact, simplicity is one reason for this updated book, which replaces the old *Angel Numbers* text. The angels want us to clearly understand their messages, which are often conveyed by repetitive number sequences. Hence, the 101 in the title of this book, as when something is referred to as "101," it's considered a primer of some sort (for example, an *English 101* course).

In *Angel Numbers 101*, I've received angelically guided meanings that are very simple, down-to-earth, and practical. This is a reference book that enables you to understand the meanings of the numbers you see, and also lets you know what to do with that information. For example, the angels are often guiding you to your next step by showing you an encouraging number such as 7. But what if you want encouragement from people around you but they aren't giving it to you?

This is what the angels have told me: "You can meditate upon any number sequence in order to bring its vibrational properties into your life."

In other words, if you'd like more abundance in your life, then draw or look at lots of number 8s. As you flip through this book, look for sequences and messages that describe your goals, desires, and intentions. Then write these numbers (and messages, if you desire) on a piece of paper where you can frequently look at it and meditate upon the numbers.

The scope of this work only goes to the number 999, but if you see a sequence with 4 or more digits, you can still use this book to ascertain its meaning. Just break the number sequence into 2- or 3-digit sequences and then look them up in this book. Your message is the accumulation of all of the smaller number sequences.

For example, if you keep seeing the number sequence 219524, you'd break it into smaller chunks of 1, 2, or 3 digits. In this case, your sequence would be 219 and 524. So, first look up the first three digits (219) in this book:

219

Your thoughts are focused on career and your purpose right now. Optimism brings the rewards you seek, so stay positive.

Next, you'd look up the second set of three digits (524):

524

Angels and archangels are watching over your new projects and helping you transform your ideas and dreams into reality.

Then, blend the meanings of both 3-digit sequences together:

> *Your thoughts are focused on career and your purpose right now. Optimism brings the rewards you seek, so stay positive. Angels and archangels are watching over your new projects and helping you transform your ideas and dreams into reality.*

In other words, you and your career are watched over by angels, so you have a very legitimate reason to feel and think optimistically about your occupation. And the more positive and optimistic you are, the better everything goes for you and everything in your life.

Since the angels give you guidance with respect to every area of your life, as you read the meaning of number sequences, notice your inner dialogue, as well as your thoughts, visions, and feelings, because this is how your angels personalize their messages. So while you're absorbing the general meaning of a number sequence, your angels will whisper exactly how that message applies to you.

Here are some explanations of the phrases used throughout this book:

Ascended masters: Great spiritual teachers who have ascended, and who are helping you and everyone else from their Heavenly perspective. These teachers are often associated with world religions, so the ascended master with whom you work is likely aligned with your spiritual or religious preferences. For instance, Christians may work with Jesus; Jews with Moses; Buddhists with Buddha or Quan Yin; Hindus with Shiva or Ganesh; and so forth. Ultimately, though, I've found that ascended masters (like angels) are nondenominational and will work with anyone who sincerely calls for their help.

Divine mission or **purpose:** Usually a spiritually based career or type of volunteer work that involves an issue you're passionate about—for instance, being a healer, teacher, or activist.

Many people find it useful to carry this book in their car or pocketbook, since the angels talk to us with numbers all throughout the day. I've heard from lots of folks who tell me how enjoyable it is to notice number sequences and then read their meanings while sitting in traffic, or other places where you're apt to see a lot of numbers.

May you enjoy talking to your angels through the fascinating world of number sequences!

With love,
Doreen Virtue

Author's Note: You may notice that some number sequences have similar meanings, especially when they're in close proximity to each other. This is due to the very subtle changes that occur as we progress along any path, goal, or intention. Progress usually comes in baby-step increments, and the angel numbers are here to encourage you all along the way. Me, too!

THE GENERAL MEANING OF NUMBERS 0 THROUGH 999

❖ 0 ❖

God is talking to you. When you see a zero, it's a sign of the endless circle of Omega without beginning or end. God is trying to get your attention with a word of reassurance or Divine guidance.

∴ 1 ∴

Stay positive. Everything you're thinking about right now is coming true, so be sure that you're only thinking about what you desire. Give any fears to God and the angels.

∴ 2 ∴

Everything's fine and will continue to be so. Keep believing, especially since your feelings of hope lead to more positive outcomes. The angels can buoy your faith if you'll ask for their help.

∴ 3 ∴

The ascended masters are helping you—usually this means an ascended master you feel close to— for example, Jesus, Quan Yin, a saint, or some other spiritual/religious figure.

∴ 4 ∴

The angels are with you. They send you the number 4 to reassure you that they've heard your prayers and are helping you.

⁙ 5 ⁙

A significant change is occurring, always for the better. It's a good idea to call upon Heaven for help with life changes.

⁙ 6 ⁙

Don't worry or obsess about material items, including money. Worry lowers the effectiveness of your prayers. Fortunately, the angels can answer your prayers if you ask them to.

⁙ 7 ⁙

You're on the right path, and the outcome will exceed your expectations! The number 7 is a sign that Divine magic is supporting you and opening doors of opportunity.

⁙ 8 ⁙

The number 8 signifies abundance and prosperity. The endless loops in this number signify an infinite flow of money, time, ideas, or whatever else you require (especially for your life purpose).

⁙ 9 ⁙

Get to work, Lightworker—now! The number 9 means that you've completed all of the prerequisites to achieve your life purpose. Stop procrastinating, as it's time to start taking action steps. Even baby steps are useful.

⁙ 10 ⁙

God wants you to hold positive thoughts about this situation, as everything is working out for your highest good. Call upon God to help you stay optimistic, as your thoughts are an influencing factor in the outcome.

⁙ 11 ⁙

Stay positive! Your thoughts are materializing rapidly, so you want to ensure positive outcomes by focusing only on the good within yourself, others, and this situation.

⁙ 12 ⁙

Keep your thoughts positive about the future, as what you are thinking influences your future. This is a message to keep your faith and hope strong, because these are strong determining factors right now.

⁘ 13 ⁘

The ascended masters (such as Jesus, Quan Yin, and so on) are with you, helping you maintain a positive outlook. The number 13 signifies that female ascended masters and goddesses are assisting you in staying positive.

⁘ 14 ⁘

Lean upon the angels to help you maintain a positive outlook. This will keep your own demeanor optimistic and bright.

⁘ 15 ⁘

As you go through changes in your life, stay positive. Your optimistic thoughts help you manifest the best outcomes with respect to these changes.

⁘ 16 ⁘

Your words are magnetic affirmations that draw to you the very things you talk and think about.

For this reason, the angels remind you to be aware of your words and thoughts.

⁙ 17 ⁙

The angels applaud you for staying positive and optimistic. They say that your optimism is warranted, as your affirmative thoughts are coming true. Keep up the good work, as you're on the right path!

⁙ 18 ⁙

Your thoughts are the valve that opens and shuts your financial flow. As you stay positive, all the material resources you need come to you easily. However, worry can stop this flow, so ask your angels to help you stay upbeat, especially where it concerns money.

⁙ 19 ⁙

This is a message for you to believe in yourself and your life purpose. The angels want you to know that you are qualified and ready to follow your dreams. Stay positive, and take action without delay.

⊹ 20 ⊹

Your connection with the Creator is strong and clear. God asks you to fill your heart and mind with faith (ask Heaven for help in doing so if you desire). Your faith is being rewarded right now.

⊹ 21 ⊹

Your optimism is definitely warranted! The angels are working behind the scenes on your behalf right this very minute. You can help support the angels' work by saying positive affirmations and believing that your dream is already manifesting.

⊹ 22 ⊹

The angels can see the positive results of your prayers, and they want you to have patience and stay optimistic while the final details are being worked out in Heaven. This is an urgent call from the angels to "keep the faith"!

⊹ 23 ⊹

You are working closely with one or more ascended masters such as Jesus, Moses, the saints, or the goddesses. This is a message from your ascended-master guides, who can see that the answer to your prayers is within reach. They encourage you to stay positive to ensure that you attract the best possible outcome.

❖ 24 ❖

Additional angels are surrounding you right now, helping you stay optimistic no matter what is going on around you. The angels know the magical power of faith, and they're releasing any negative thoughts and emotions to give you a clear path for the manifestation of your desires.

❖ 25 ❖

As you go through major life changes, expect the best and your optimism will be rewarded.

❖ 26 ❖

Positive affirmations help your situation improve quickly. The angels urge you to only think and speak about your desires, and not to affirm your fears, as they are just an illusion.

⁜ 27 ⁜

Congratulations! Your optimism is attracting wonderful situations and relationships. Stay positive, as this attitude is working in your favor.

⁜ 28 ⁜

Money comes to you as you keep the faith that you, your loved ones, and your beautiful life purpose are all fully supported by Heaven.

⁜ 29 ⁜

Stay positive about your life purpose, and put all of your focus on being of service, utilizing your natural talents, passions, and interests. Doors are opening for you. Just keep your faith strong.

⁜ 30 ⁜

You are fully supported by God and the ascended masters. Step forward confidently in the direction of your dreams!

⸭ 31 ⸭

The ascended masters ask you to look past all earthly illusions and see the Divine perfection within you, other people, and your current situation. As you see Divine perfection in your mind, it manifests externally in your relationships, career, health, and other life areas.

⸭ 32 ⸭

The ascended master Jesus reminds you to apply his affirmation about the power of faith ("With faith, all things are possible") to your own life right now.

⸭ 33 ⸭

You have a strong and clear connection with one or more ascended masters, who have answered your call and your prayers. Keep talking to them, as they're helping you with your present situation.

⸭ 34 ⸭

Your prayers are heard and answered by the angels and ascended masters, who are with you right now.

✢ 35 ✢

A positive change is coming about for you, with the assistance and protection of the ascended masters.

✢ 36 ✢

The ascended masters ask you to keep your thoughts focused on spirit, and release any material worries to them.

✢ 37 ✢

You are on the right path, and the ascended masters are encouraging and helping you along the way.

✢ 38 ✢

The ascended masters are helping you with your financial situation.

✢ 39 ✢

You are being helped by the ascended masters, who are strongly encouraging you to work on your life purpose right now.

∴ 40 ∴

God and the angels are surrounding you with Heavenly love and protection.

∴ 41 ∴

The angels ask you to keep very positive thoughts, as everything you say and think is manifesting into form rapidly.

∴ 42 ∴

The angels are urging you to keep the faith!

∴ 43 ∴

Both the angels and the ascended masters (such as Jesus, Quan Yin, or a saint) are helping you right now. Spend time connecting with them in quiet meditation, and be calmed by their reassuring presence, which tells you that everything is fine.

∴ 44 ∴

The angels are giving you extra comfort, love, and support right now. Ask them for help with everything, and listen to their guidance through your intuition.

⸭ 45 ⸭

The angels are helping you through a positive life change.

⸭ 46 ⸭

The angels are saying to you: "Keep your thoughts focused upon your spiritual self and your Divine Source for everything. Give any material worries to us."

⸭ 47 ⸭

The angels say that you are on the right path. Keep up the good work!

⸭ 48 ⸭

Your prayers about money have been heard and answered by the angels.

⁙ 49 ⁙

The angels urge you to get to work on your major goals and life purpose without delay. Ask them to help you with ideas, courage, and motivation.

⁙ 50 ⁙

God is helping you to change your life in healthful new ways.

⁙ 51 ⁙

Keep positive thoughts about the changes you're desiring and experiencing.

⁙ 52 ⁙

Have faith that the changes you're considering or experiencing are for the best.

⁙ 53 ⁙

The ascended masters are helping you change your life in positive ways. Ask for their help with any aspect of these situations, such as additional ideas, opportunities, courage, and so forth.

⁙ 54 ⁙

The angels are guiding and supporting you as you make healthy and necessary changes in your life.

⁙ 55 ⁙

This is a period of "out with the old, in with the new." Welcome these changes, as they bring about new blessings.

⁙ 56 ⁙

As you go through changes with your home life, career, and relationships, stay focused on your inner spirit's growth. Find the blessing within each change you're experiencing.

⁙ 57 ⁙

The changes you are experiencing are for the best. Trust these changes to lead you where you want to go.

⸭ 58 ⸭

Your finances are improving, and there will be a positive change in your financial flow. This could also signal a job promotion or career change, with an increased salary.

⸭ 59 ⸭

The changes you are going through are bringing you closer to your Divine life purpose. You can calm anxieties by spending time on activities related to your spiritual interests.

⸭ 60 ⸭

You are vacillating between focusing upon Spirit and the material world. This number is a call for you to balance your focus, and always remember that Spirit is your source and the force behind everything in your life.

⸭ 61 ⸭

Keep your thoughts about your material life (such as home, work, body, and possessions) very positively focused. Your thoughts are affecting your life, so only think about your desires and not about any fears.

⁜ 62 ⁜

Keep believing that the details of your life are working out in miraculous ways. Your faith opens the door for miracles!

⁜ 63 ⁜

The ascended masters are helping you with the daily aspects of your life. Ask them for help, and then be open to receiving the assistance that they bring to you in the form of ideas, guidance, and unexpected gifts.

⁜ 64 ⁜

You are fully supported by the angels in every area of your life. Give any fears or worries to the angels, and ask them for any assistance that you need right now.

⁜ 65 ⁜

Congratulations on the positive changes you're making in your life right now. This is an excellent time to make changes at home, work, or within relationships. Follow your inner truth.

⁘ 66 ⁘

When you're burdened by worries, stress, or fear, it's more difficult to hear your angels' loving help. This is a message for you to spend time in prayer and meditation. Ask for spiritual intervention, and open your arms to receive the help that always follows prayers.

⁘ 67 ⁘

Well done! You're on the right path at home and at work.

⁘ 68 ⁘

Remember that Spirit is the source of your income. Worry doesn't assist you with your finances, but prayer always helps every part of your life.

⁘ 69 ⁘

As you spend time working on activities related to your spiritual passions and interests, every part of your life automatically improves.

⁘ 70 ⁘

This is a message from God that you're on the right path. Keep up the good work!

⁘ 71 ⁘

You are on track with your desires and manifestations. Just stay positive and optimistic, and all of your dreams will be right there for you.

⁘ 72 ⁘

Have faith that you're taking the right steps toward the manifestation of your desires . . . because you are!

⁘ 73 ⁘

The ascended masters are guiding you, and you are listening to them accurately. Stay on your present path, as it is illuminated with blessings and gifts.

⁘ 74 ⁘

The angels surround you and walk beside you every step of the way. You're on the fast track to the manifestation of your dreams, so stick to the ideas and activities you're involved with now.

∴ 75 ∴

The changes you're making or considering are exactly right for you.

∴ 76 ∴

You're on the right path, and your material needs are fully supported by your choices and actions.

∴ 77 ∴

Keep up the great work! Everything you're doing right now has the Midas touch!

∴ 78 ∴

Your present focus and actions have tapped into the Universal financial flow of abundance. Stick with your current plans, as they're right on the money.

⁜ 79 ⁜

You're on the right path for your Divine life purpose.

⁜ 80 ⁜

God is supporting you in all areas, including your financial life. Let go and let God help you.

⁜ 81 ⁜

The more you stay positive about money, the greater your financial flow will be.

⁜ 82 ⁜

Keep the faith that your financial situation is taken care of. Give any worries to God and the angels.

⁜ 83 ⁜

The ascended masters have heard and answered your prayers about your financial needs.

⋰ 84 ⋰

The angels are helping you increase your financial flow so that you attain a state of security and abundance.

⋰ 85 ⋰

Hooray! You're experiencing positive changes in your financial situation.

⋰ 86 ⋰

Keep your thoughts about money spiritually based, and let go of earthly concerns about finances. The higher your thoughts, the better your financial flow.

⋰ 87 ⋰

You're on the right track with respect to your career and finances. Keep going!

⋰ 88 ⋰

This is a very auspicious and favorable sign about your finances. Your actions, prayers, visualizations, and manifestation work have resulted in a large inflow of abundance. Open your arms and receive!

❖ 89 ❖

Your Divine life purpose is key to opening the door to abundance. Take steps daily (beginning now) to work in areas related to your spiritual passions and interests. These areas are the foundation of your Divine life purpose.

❖ 90 ❖

God is calling upon you to work on your Divine life mission without delay. You are ready! Take action today, doing something related to your spiritual interests.

❖ 91 ❖

Stay positive and optimistic about your Divine life purpose. You and your mission are needed in this world.

⁜ 92 ⁜

As you keep the faith that everything is unfolding perfectly with your Divine life purpose, you more clearly see and understand the steps that are best for you to take.

⁜ 93 ⁜

The ascended masters are guiding, protecting, and supporting you. Because you've listened to their guidance (even unconsciously), you're now on the right path for the fruition of your dreams and life purpose.

⁜ 94 ⁜

Your actions are guided and supported by the angels, who say that you're doing great—keep up the good work!

⁜ 95 ⁜

The changes that you're currently considering are taking you in the right direction for the manifestation of your Divine life purpose.

⁖ 96 ⁖

With respect to your Divine life purpose, put all of your focus onto the spiritual aspects (such as helping others, asking for Heaven to support you, and coming from a place of love). Give any earthly concerns about your purpose to God and the angels.

⁖ 97 ⁖

Keep trusting and following your intuition, as it's right on the mark.

⁖ 98 ⁖

The more that you focus, and take action upon, your Divine life purpose, the more that the gateways of abundance open up for you. Focus on your purpose, and let your finances take care of themselves.

⁖ 99 ⁖

The spirit world has an urgent message for you: "Get to work on your Divine life purpose now!" Ask the spirit world to help you with motivation, clarity, direction, and anything else you need.

·:· 100 ·:·

This is a strong message from God, telling you that your positive thoughts are necessary to co-create the outcome you desire.

·:· 101 ·:·

This number signifies fundamental spiritual teachings: As you "let go and let God," your thoughts automatically become more positive, and this elevated vibration attracts all good things into your life.

·:· 102 ·:·

All of your prayers and positive thoughts are sprouting into your desired form! Give any worries to God, and stay filled with faith, as you'll soon see a positive outcome.

·:· 103 ·:·

The more that you stay optimistic, the more easily God and the ascended masters (such as the saints, Jesus, and so on) can help you.

☩ 104 ☩

You are surrounded by the love of God and the angels, who are lifting you up to a happier level. You can speed up this effect by maintaining a positive outlook.

☩ 105 ☩

As you change your life for the better, you're supported by God's powerful and loving energy. Give any worries to God, because your positive thoughts act like angels along the way.

☩ 106 ☩

The more you focus on God's love and wisdom, the more you tap into this source of strength and support. "Seek ye first the kingdom of God and all will be added unto you."

☩ 107 ☩

You've been listening to God's loving guidance, and as a result, you're exactly where you're supposed to be.

⁜ 108 ⁜

Your positive thoughts and prayerful connection with God's infinite love have yielded an unending flow of abundance for you.

⁜ 109 ⁜

This is a strong message to stay optimistic about your Divine life mission, as well as to take steady action in the direction of your dreams.

⁜ 110 ⁜

You and God are co-creating the answers to your prayers, and God needs your cooperation in this endeavor. Help Him by staying positive and following Divine guidance.

⁜ 111 ⁜

This number brings you the urgent message that your thoughts are manifesting instantly, so keep your mind-set focused upon your desires. Give any fearful thoughts to Heaven for transmutation.

⁘ 112 ⁘

Faith and optimism are the two factors that unlock the doors to all of your desires.

⁘ 113 ⁘

The ascended masters are buoying your thoughts so that you will expect the miracles that are coming to you.

⁘ 114 ⁘

Ask the angels to help you stay optimistic, as they're urging you to keep your thoughts at the highest vibrational levels.

⁘ 115 ⁘

The more that you hold positive thoughts about the changes you're currently making or considering, the better the outcome will be for you and everyone involved.

⁘ 116 ⁘

Hold the highest vision for your material life (such as career, home, and lifestyle), because your thoughts are manifesting into form in these life areas.

⁙ 117 ⁙

Congratulations! Your positive thoughts have steered you and your life in a wonderful direction. Keep up the positive mental work.

⁙ 118 ⁙

Your positive thoughts about money have opened the doors to increased financial flow. Stay optimistic, because it's working!

⁙ 119 ⁙

Keep your thoughts and feelings concerning your Divine life purpose as high-vibrating and positive as possible. Your thoughts are steering your experiences with respect to your purpose.

⁙ 120 ⁙

Beautiful! You've centered your entire mind and heart upon the positive energy of God's love.

∻ 121 ∻

Now is the time for your unwavering faith and optimism, which always yield the highest possible outcome for you.

∻ 122 ∻

Stay filled with faith, because Heaven is working behind the scenes to help your manifestations appear. The more positive your thoughts and feelings, the faster and better this manifestation occurs.

∻ 123 ∻

Simplify your life by letting go of anything extraneous or unnecessary. Ask others (including Heaven) to help you, and delegate more often.

∻ 124 ∻

The angels are helping you stay positive by lifting your thoughts to the energy of Divine love.

⁘ 125 ⁘

All of the changes that you've been making or considering will go much more smoothly if you keep a positive mind-set.

⁘ 126 ⁘

The more you stay positive and filled with faith, the better the outcome of your current situation. You're steering the ship with your thoughts, so keep them uplifted.

⁘ 127 ⁘

You're on the right path, so your optimism is warranted. Stay positive and keep doing what you're doing!

⁘ 128 ⁘

The more you keep your mind and body filled with positive energies, the more the gateways of abundance open widely for you.

⊹ 129 ⊹

Your Divine life mission is important and very needed in the world. Stay positive and take daily action steps related to your spiritual passions and interests.

⊹ 130 ⊹

God and the ascended masters are working with you to lift your thoughts and energies so that they're centered and loving.

⊹ 131 ⊹

Ask the ascended masters for help with whatever you're experiencing or desiring right now. They will boost your confidence and courage.

⊹ 132 ⊹

Most stories of ascended masters (such as Jesus, Moses, and Buddha) talk about their incredible faith, which caused miracles to occur. Well, this number is a message from the masters who are helping you boost your faith Heavenward.

⊹ 133 ⊹

You have nothing to fear or worry about, as the ascended masters are completely supporting and surrounding you in all ways.

⊹ 134 ⊹

You have a great deal of spiritual support right now. Give any cares or concerns to the angels and ascended masters, who are lovingly surrounding you right now.

⊹ 135 ⊹

Your positive thoughts and the support of the ascended masters have spurred the healthy changes that you're experiencing. Trust these changes to lead you to the answers to your prayers.

⊹ 136 ⊹

Your prayers and requests for help with your material needs have been heard and answered. All you need to do is keep your thoughts focused on your dreams, and release any fears to the ascended masters.

⁘ 137 ⁘

You've done it! Your prayers and visualizations have put you on the right path. Just keep following your guidance and keep affirming a positive outcome.

⁘ 138 ⁘

Stick with your positive affirmations and prayers regarding your career and finances, and continue to give away any worries or concerns to the ascended masters, who surround you with love.

⁘ 139 ⁘

Keep visualizing yourself happily on the path of your Divine life mission, and continue praying and conversing with the ascended masters. They are here to support you with your mission.

⁘ 140 ⁘

God and the angels are boosting your thoughts to a very positive level so that you can continue attracting all good things into your life.

⁘ 141 ⁘

This is a strong message from the angels, urging you to turn your thoughts away from worries. Instead, use prayer and positive affirmations to focus your thoughts on optimistic visions of your desired outcome.

⁘ 142 ⁘

The angels are helping you stay strong, positive, and filled with faith. They know that this situation is working out beautifully, and they want you to know that everything's okay.

⁘ 143 ⁘

There's no need to worry; the ascended masters and angels are right by your side, assuring you of a positive outcome.

⁘ 144 ⁘

The angels are urging you to keep your thoughts positive, as your optimism attracts the highest good. Ask the angels for help with releasing fears, and it is done.

❖ 145 ❖

Yes, the changes you're considering making are Divinely guided. You can deal with these issues confidently, knowing that the angels are helping you all along the way.

❖ 146 ❖

Your positive affirmations are ensuring that all of your physical needs are met. The angels urge you to continue your prayers, visualizations, and other manifestation processes.

❖ 147 ❖

You're thinking clearly about this situation, and you're on the right path in your decisions and actions. The angels are protecting you.

❖ 148 ❖

The angels are helping you with your career and finances. You can feel this help, and are beginning to relax and feel better about your financial needs.

⁜ 149 ⁜

Rest easy about your Divinely guided career, as the angels are giving you a wealth of information and ideas. Just trust and follow these ideas and everything else will take care of itself.

⁜ 150 ⁜

As you go through this period of change, know that you are lovingly supported by God and also by your positive intentions.

⁜ 151 ⁜

It's very important that you approach any changes you're considering with a very positive mind-set. Your thoughts determine the outcome of these changes.

⁜ 152 ⁜

Approach new ideas, situations, and relationships with an open mind, and allow yourself to try novel methods.

⁘ 153 ⁘

It's safe for you to make the changes that you're considering. As long as you stay focused upon service and Divine love—which the ascended masters can help you do—these changes will be fortuitous.

⁘ 154 ⁘

The angels are here to help you make necessary changes, which will increase your level of happiness and satisfaction. Ask for Heaven's help, especially with respect to maintaining a positive mind-set.

⁘ 155 ⁘

It's essential that you make some positive changes in your life. You've had enough of the present situation, and now it's time to take charge and do things your way.

⁘ 156 ⁘

Your determination to positively change your career, finances, home, or other earthly matters is a Divinely guided idea.

❖ 157 ❖

You're on the right path with your new ideas and activities. Keep them up!

❖ 158 ❖

Your new focus on attracting and manifesting an increased income is working. As you continue your positive affirmations and visualizations, you experience increased abundance.

❖ 159 ❖

This is a perfect time to begin work on an aspect of your Divine life purpose. Choose the first action step that comes to mind, related to your spiritual interests.

❖ 160 ❖

God has heard and answered your prayers, and you can co-create the answers faster by monitoring your speech and thoughts so that you're always describing yourself and your situation in positive terms.

⁙ 161 ⁙

This is a strong message urging you to keep positive thoughts with respect to your finances, career, home, and other earthly issues. These positive thoughts will carry you far.

⁙ 162 ⁙

Stay strong and centered in faith, as your prayers regarding your material needs manifest into form.

⁙ 163 ⁙

The ascended masters have heard and answered your prayers for help. All you need to do to receive your answered prayer is use positive words in your thoughts and speech.

⁙ 164 ⁙

The angels are lifting away old worries and concerns so that your life can improve in miraculous ways.

❖ 165 ❖

You are fully supported as you change your career, home, relationships, and other life areas. These changes are for the best.

❖ 166 ❖

It's vital that you use only positive words to think and speak about your career, home, and relationships. The words that you use determine your future, so choose well.

❖ 167 ❖

You're on the right path to improving your life, as long as you keep a positive vision of your desired outcome.

❖ 168 ❖

The key to increasing your financial flow is to use only positive words to describe and think about money.

⠇ 169 ⠇

The intuitive push to work on your Divine life mission is real. Visualize and affirm often: *I am happily fulfilling my Divine life mission now,* to make it a reality.

⠇ 170 ⠇

Congratulations on using affirmations, prayers, and other manifestation tools, as they're working for you!

⠇ 171 ⠇

You deserve the happiness and success you're experiencing. It's safe for you to be happy and successful, so relax and enjoy it.

⠇ 172 ⠇

Trust that your choices are Divinely guided, because they are.

⠇ 173 ⠇

You're walking along the right path, with the ascended masters (such as the saints, Jesus, Quan

Yin, and so forth) as your companions, protectors, and guides.

∴ 174 ∴

You've listened accurately to your guardian angels' Divine guidance, and as a result, you're on the right track for your purpose and the manifestation of your dreams into reality.

∴ 175 ∴

You are correctly making changes that will enhance your life greatly.

∴ 176 ∴

You're on the right path to improving your life so that your material needs are more easily met.

∴ 177 ∴

You're in an auspicious period of your life, where your intentions are all manifesting in very positive ways. Choose what you think and speak about carefully, as your words are like orders that you place with the Universe . . . and that's what will be delivered to you.

⁘ 178 ⁘

All of your positive thoughts and affirmations have resulted in an increased flow of financial abundance. Keep it up!

⁘ 179 ⁘

You're on the right path for your Divine life purpose. Continue with your visualizations and expect a happy outcome, as your expectations are determining your future.

⁘ 180 ⁘

Your positive thoughts and prayers are bringing forth an increased flow of financial abundance.

⁘ 181 ⁘

To heal your financial situation, use positive affirmations and visualize your abundance.

∴ 182 ∴

Your career and finances are completely dependent upon your mental outlook. If you're happy and filled with trust and faith with respect to your success, then that's what you'll easily experience.

∴ 183 ∴

The ascended masters are guiding you through your meditations and intuition, especially in the areas of career and finance.

∴ 184 ∴

Your guardian angels are watching over you, and they're encouraging you to give them any worries or cares about your career and financial situation.

∴ 185 ∴

The changes that you're considering making bring positive effects to your financial situation.

∴ 186 ∴

It's more important than ever for you to use your manifestation tools such as positive affirmations, visualization, and prayers to consciously heal your finances and other areas where you desire abundance.

⁖ 187 ⁖

Follow your inner guidance in your career choices, as you're tapped into accurate information that will fully support you.

⁖ 188 ⁖

Well done! All of your meditating and visualizing have opened the floodgates to increased financial flow.

⁖ 189 ⁖

Trust that you will be fully financially supported as you devote your time and energy to your Divine life purpose (which consists of spiritual topics that you feel passionate about).

⁖ 190 ⁖

You're being called upon to devote yourself to working on your Divine mission. Visualize yourself happily working in a meaningful career, and

know that this will come about as you steadily
follow your inner guidance.

⚜ 191 ⚜

Your positive thoughts are opening doors to the
fruition of your dream career and Divine life purpose. Step through these doors without delay.

⚜ 192 ⚜

Trust that you are ready for your Divine life purpose, and that it is much needed in this world.
You are ready and qualified to fulfill this mission.

⚜ 193 ⚜

The ascended masters (such as the saints, Jesus,
Buddha, and so forth) are supporting you and
your Divine life mission. Give them any cares you
may have concerning your career.

⚜ 194 ⚜

The angels have heard your prayers concerning
your career and finding your Divine mission in
life. They are helping you by giving you guidance

through your intuition and dreams, and in other subtle ways. Listen to and follow this guidance.

⁙ 195 ⁙

The changes that you are making are well timed. You are clear about what you will and won't accept in your life. These changes put you on the path of your Divine mission . . . and will result in you helping others to do the same.

⁙ 196 ⁙

Give any cares or worries concerning your career or purpose to Spirit, as your positive thoughts are a determining factor in these situations.

⁙ 197 ⁙

You're on the right path with respect to your career and purpose. Keep up the positive affirmations, as they're working!

⁙ 198 ⁙

Your life purpose is the answer to your prayers about money. Devote yourself to service that involves your natural talents and interests, and you will be fully supported in return.

⸭ 199 ⸭

It's essential that you hold positive thoughts about your career and Divine life mission, as your thoughts are determining the outcome.

⸭ 200 ⸭

God's powerful and unconditional love is filling your heart and mind with faith so that you can rise above any seeming troubles. Trust that all is well, because it is.

⸭ 201 ⸭

You are co-creating the answers to your prayers with the words that you say, think, and write. This is a message for you to choose loving and positive words so that your outcome is both loving and positive.

⸭ 202 ⸭

God is helping to boost your faith, because with faith everything is possible.

⁜ 203 ⁜

All of your prayers are heard and answered. The more you believe this, the better and faster the outcome. Trust.

⁜ 204 ⁜

Angels surround you with God's healing love. Open your heart and mind to receive this Divine gift, which is bringing blessings to you.

⁜ 205 ⁜

Your faith and prayerful devotion has resulted in positive life changes. Trust that these changes are answers to your prayers.

⁜ 206 ⁜

Your prayers and faith are supporting you and your material needs completely. Turn any worries into prayers, and be open to receiving the *answers* to those prayers.

∴ 207 ∴

The Universe is patting you on the back, applauding the way you've lived on a foundation of prayer and spiritual devotion. Keep up the good work!

∴ 208 ∴

Your positive outlook, prayers, and other manifestation activities have created financial security for you. Expect an increase in funds, such as a raise, promotion, or windfall.

∴ 209 ∴

You've been praying about your Divine life purpose, and the answer is: "Walk confidently in faith, in the direction of your intuition and spiritual passions. Trust that you are fully supported upon this path."

∴ 210 ∴

You are co-creating the answers to your prayers, and their outcome is determined by your faith that everything is already healed in spiritual truth. Trust that all is well, and it is.

⁑ 211 ⁑

Now is the time for you to rise above any seeming problems; and ensure that every word you speak, write, or think is as positive as possible. You are manifesting very quickly, so you want to ensure that you focus solely upon your desired outcomes and do not dwell upon any fears.

⁑ 212 ⁑

The more you believe, the better everything turns out. Believe and trust!

⁑ 213 ⁑

The ascended masters, especially the goddesses, are helping you see this situation from a perspective of Divine love. The more you can see this situation through the eyes of love, the better the outcome.

⁑ 214 ⁑

You are supported by the archangels and angels. Give them any cares or worries, because as your mind is illuminated with joy and faith, you attract more favorable outcomes.

⊹ 215 ⊹

You've been focusing upon changing your life, and that positive change is now upon you. Trust that this change is for the best, because it is.

⊹ 216 ⊹

Your material needs are more easily met when you hold a positive mind-set. Like attracts like.

⊹ 217 ⊹

You've done a lot of great spiritual, emotional, and mental work on yourself with positive and effective results. Well done!

⊹ 218 ⊹

The angels say that your thoughts are steering the direction of your finances. Positive thoughts steer you in positive directions.

⊹ 219 ⊹

Your thoughts are focused on career and your purpose right now. Optimism brings the rewards you seek, so stay positive.

⚜ 220 ⚜

This is a strong Divine message urging you to hold on to hope, trust, and faith, as these qualities determine the outcome of your current situation.

⚜ 221 ⚜

The more you can stay positive (in your thoughts, speech, actions, and written words), the better this experience will be for you and your loved ones.

⚜ 222 ⚜

Trust that everything is working out exactly as it's supposed to, with Divine blessings for everyone involved. Let go and have faith.

⚜ 223 ⚜

A healing miracle is imminent, engendered by your faith and your clear connection to one or more ascended masters who have heard and answered your prayers.

⁜ 224 ⁜

The angels are boosting your confidence, faith, and trust, as these qualities help them answer your prayers.

⁜ 225 ⁜

You are becoming more positive in the way that you think, act, speak, and write. This new positive energy is boosting your life.

⁜ 226 ⁜

Your faith determines your flow of material supply (such as money, home, and other earthly needs). The more positive you are, the greater your flow of good.

⁜ 227 ⁜

Your awesome faith and positive outlook are being rewarded by the infallible Law of Attraction.

⚜ 228 ⚜

Trust that new opportunities are answers to your prayers. Walk through the doors that are opening for you, and accept offers of help.

⚜ 229 ⚜

Know that your Divine life purpose is unique and much needed. Trust that you're fulfilling this purpose right this very minute. No one can do this but you.

⚜ 230 ⚜

You have a clear connection with Heaven, especially during moments of peace when you feel the certainty that God and the ascended masters are watching over you (because they are!).

⚜ 231 ⚜

"With faith, all things are possible," the ascended masters are reminding you. Ask them to increase your faith if you feel that it's wavering.

❖ 232 ❖

Don't focus on problems or lack, but instead stay centered in prayer and faith that you are protected, loved, and watched over by powerful ascended masters.

❖ 233 ❖

You've asked for the help of many ascended masters, and they are with you right now, just as you've requested.

❖ 234 ❖

You have powerful allies in the angels, archangels, and ascended masters. They are with you right now, helping and guiding you.

❖ 235 ❖

Your prayers to change your life have been heard and answered by the ascended masters, who are helping you rearrange your life in healthy ways.

⁑ 236 ⁑

Your earthly needs for home, shelter, and so forth are being provided for by the ascended masters in response to your prayers and unwavering faith.

⁑ 237 ⁑

Your prayers, meditations, and other spiritual practices have aligned you with the loving energy of the ascended masters.

⁑ 238 ⁑

The ascended masters have heard and answered your prayers for increased abundance. They know that we humans have material needs, which they are helping you with right now.

⁑ 239 ⁑

You and your Divine life purpose are being helped by powerful ascended masters. Ask them for guidance with respect to the next step on your career path, and they will directly guide you.

⚜ 240 ⚜

God and the angels are boosting your self-esteem, confidence, and faith. Be open to their help.

⚜ 241 ⚜

Your connection to the angels is opening your heart to the powerfully healing energy of love. Keep talking to the angels, as they are blessing you and your life.

⚜ 242 ⚜

This is a strong message from the angels, asking you to trust that everything is okay and working out in Divine and perfect order. With faith, all things are possible.

⚜ 243 ⚜

Your prayers have been heard and answered by the angels and ascended masters. Trust, and give any cares or worries to them.

⁖ 244 ⁖

You are surrounded by powerful angels who love you unconditionally. There is nothing to fear.

⁖ 245 ⁖

The angels have helped you orchestrate positive changes, which are bringing great blessings into your life.

⁖ 246 ⁖

Your prayers for help with your material needs (such as money, home, transportation, and so forth) have been heard and answered by the angels.

⁖ 247 ⁖

The angels say that all of your prayers are being rewarded. Keep the faith!

⁖ 248 ⁖

Your connection with the angels is very deep and clear. They are intimately connected to every area of your life, including your career and finances.

⁖ 249 ⁖

You've been receiving angelic messages about your Divine life purpose. This guidance may appear as intuitive feelings, or a deep desire to serve in ways connected to your passionate interests. Trust this guidance and act upon it without delay.

⁖ 250 ⁖

Your prayers to positively change your life have been heard and answered. The more you stay filled with faith about these changes, the better the outcome.

⁖ 251 ⁖

You are steering the wheel of your life right now. It's essential that you stay positive about the changes you're making or considering, as that determines your destination.

⁖ 252 ⁖

Rest assured that your recent decisions are good ones. Move forward with your plans with full faith that they are right.

✧ 253 ✧

Your heartfelt prayers are the reason for the changes that you're making or considering. These changes are truly answers to your prayers, so welcome them!

✧ 254 ✧

The angels are watching over you as you change your life for the better. Ask them for help with all aspects of this change . . . and it is given.

✧ 255 ✧

Trust that the change you are experiencing is for the best, because it is.

✧ 256 ✧

You are making positive changes that will help you better provide for yourself and your loved ones.

✧ 257 ✧

Stay your course, as you are moving in the right direction.

∴ 258 ∴

Your financial life is changing for the better, mani-
fested as receiving a raise, increased financial flow
with your business, or an unexpected windfall.

∴ 259 ∴

You're changing your life so that you can fulfill
your Divine life mission. Have faith that these
changes have a spiritual purpose, because they do.

∴ 260 ∴

God has heard and answered your prayers to meet
your material needs for food, shelter, and other
supplies. Trust.

∴ 261 ∴

Your material supplies are intimately connected
to your thoughts. The more positive you are, the
easier it is for your needs to be met.

⁘ 262 ⁘

Have faith that your bills are being paid, and that you have enough for you and your family. Your faith will be promptly rewarded!

⁘ 263 ⁘

The ascended masters have heard and answered your prayers for help in meeting your needs for food, shelter, and other earthly needs.

⁘ 264 ⁘

Trust that you and your loved ones are watched over, protected, and supplied for by the angels, because you are.

⁘ 265 ⁘

The positive and healthy changes you're in the midst of make it easier for you to support yourself and your family. Relax . . . the worst is now behind you.

❖ 266 ❖

It's essential that you focus on the spiritual Source for all of your earthly needs. If you concentrate on illusions of scarcity or lack, that is what you'll attract. This is a time that calls for you to have faith, which will be promptly rewarded.

❖ 267 ❖

You're on the right path with respect to your thoughts on how to better manage or increase your finances to meet your material needs. Stay elevated in your thoughts and feelings about money and you'll experience a much easier time of it.

❖ 268 ❖

It's essential that you approach money from a spiritual perspective. Always remember that your Source is within and around you. Give thanks for an increased supply and it is done.

❖ 269 ❖

You are fully supported, and all of your material needs are met, as you devote yourself to working on your Divine life purpose.

⁜ 270 ⁜

The Universe is congratulating you on "keeping the faith," which has caused your light and love to shine radiantly.

⁜ 271 ⁜

Your faith and positive thinking are pushing you forward toward the realization of your dreams.

⁜ 272 ⁜

Trust that you're making the right move, because you are.

⁜ 273 ⁜

You're going in the right direction, thanks to your prayers and the help of beloved ascended masters.

⁜ 274 ⁜

The angels ask you to have faith in yourself and what you're doing, because it's the right thing for you.

⁜ 275 ⁜

The changes you're making will affect your life in very positive ways. Move forward confidently with your plans.

⁜ 276 ⁜

Congratulations! Your faith and decisive actions have put you squarely on the right path to improving conditions in your life.

⁜ 277 ⁜

You've prayed with devotion and have listened attentively to your Divine guidance. As you follow this guidance, you're protected, and everything you do turns to gold.

⁜ 278 ⁜

You've tapped into the secrets of abundance by visualizing prosperity and following your intuitive guidance accordingly.

⁘ 279 ⁘

Trust that you're on the right path for your Divine life purpose.

⁘ 280 ⁘

Have faith that all of your financial needs are being taken care of by God's loving attention.

⁘ 281 ⁘

The more positive you keep your thoughts and feelings concerning finances, the better everything works out.

⁘ 282 ⁘

Listen to your own inner guidance about work and finances, as your positive mind-set is giving you accurate information.

⁘ 283 ⁘

Lean upon the ascended masters with whom you feel spiritually or religiously connected to, as they will support your physical needs.

⁙ 284 ⁙

The angels are boosting your faith and your financial flow.

⁙ 285 ⁙

A positive change in your finances is imminent.

⁙ 286 ⁙

Don't worry! You will be supplied with enough money to pay all of your bills and meet all of your needs.

⁙ 287 ⁙

Everything you're doing is helping to increase your financial flow. Keep going.

⁙ 288 ⁙

Your confidence, faith, trust, and hope have opened the floodgates of abundance for you.

⁙ 289 ⁙

Trust that you'll be completely financially supported as you focus on your Divine life purpose.

⁘ 290 ⁘

Your Divine life purpose is God's will, and it is right for you to focus your time and energy upon this purpose.

⁘ 291 ⁘

Trust that you're being guided about your Divine life purpose. You don't need to know everything about your purpose now—just keeping the faith and following your intuitive guidance is all that's required.

⁘ 292 ⁘

On a daily basis, spend time visualizing yourself having a meaningful career that makes your heart sing with joy. Your visualizations help your Divine life purpose manifest into reality.

⁘ 293 ⁘

The ascended masters are urging you to focus on your mission in life, which consists of your spiritual passions and interests.

∴ 294 ∴

The angels are fully supporting you as you devote time and energy toward fulfilling your Divine mission.

∴ 295 ∴

Trust that the changes you're making or considering are adjusting your life so that you can better focus on your Divine purpose.

∴ 296 ∴

Have faith that all of your material needs for your Divine life purpose are supplied to you as you ask, and as you open your arms to receive.

∴ 297 ∴

Trust that you are on the right path of your Divine life purpose. All is well.

∴ 298 ∴

Your prayers about finding a meaningful career that yields a meaningful income have been heard and answered. As you work on your Divine life mission, everything improves, including your finances.

∴ 299 ∴

Have faith about your Divine life mission, because it is real, much needed, and you are ready to work on it now.

∴ 300 ∴

The ascended masters and God support, surround, protect, and love you unconditionally . . . now and always!

∴ 301 ∴

You are co-creating the answers to your prayers with God and the ascended masters. The more you keep your thoughts Heavenward and positive, the faster your prayers are answered.

∴ 302 ∴

Your heart is filled with faith, which has opened the doors for all of Heaven to fully help you.

✥ 303 ✥

God and the ascended masters have heard and answered your prayers.

✥ 304 ✥

Your prayers have been heard by Heaven, and they are working on your behalf right now. Give them any worries or fears, and stay positive, because everything is moving in the right direction.

✥ 305 ✥

God and the ascended masters walk right beside you through every step of the changes you're experiencing.

✥ 306 ✥

Give any concerns or worries to God and the ascended masters, who are with you right now.

✥ 307 ✥

Good for you! You've been listening to Divine guidance, and have adjusted your course of action so that you're now operating from a place of loving wisdom.

⁘ 308 ⁘

God and the ascended masters are supporting you in every area of your life, including your career and finances.

⁘ 309 ⁘

Because you've been listening to Heaven's loving wisdom, you're now embarking on your Divine life purpose of service to the world.

⁘ 310 ⁘

This is a strong message from the spirit world asking you to keep your thoughts high, bright, and positive. God and the ascended masters will help you lift your thoughts Heavenward, if you'll ask for their help with this.

⁘ 311 ⁘

Because you're surrounded by so many wise and loving ascended masters, your energy and thoughts have been lifted to a level of instant manifestation. Keep your thoughts centered upon positive and loving topics.

❖ 312 ❖

Heaven is helping you stay positive and filled with faith, which are two key qualities that allow the ascended masters to fully answer your prayers.

❖ 313 ❖

Lean upon the positive and loving energies of the ascended masters who surround you right now, as they're lifting your thoughts to higher levels of happy living.

❖ 314 ❖

Your success is guaranteed, as you're surrounded by angels and ascended masters. All you need to do is keep your thoughts focused on your desired outcomes.

❖ 315 ❖

The ascended masters are helping you to be brave, strong, and optimistic as you change your life for the better.

✢ 316 ✢

You are working with powerful ascended masters, who are supporting your material needs. Trust and be open to receiving their support, which is always available to you.

✢ 317 ✢

The ascended masters congratulate you on your recent decisions and actions. They ask you to stay positive as you continue along your golden new pathway.

✢ 318 ✢

You've prayed for help about finances, and the ascended masters have heard and answered these prayers. All that's needed from you is an optimistic mind-set, as you follow the intuitive guidance that Heaven is sending to you.

✢ 319 ✢

The ascended masters are giving you ideas and thoughts about your Divine life guidance. Pay attention to, and follow through with, these ideas because they're answers to your prayers about your mission in life.

⊹ 320 ⊹

God and the ascended masters are surrounding you with supportive and healing love, helping you to have confidence that everything is in Divine and perfect order.

⊹ 321 ⊹

Give any concerns to the ascended masters (such as the saints, Jesus, Buddha, and so forth), and they will replace your fears with faith.

⊹ 322 ⊹

This is a strong message from the ascended masters, urging you to "keep the faith," and thus experience faith's magical magnetic power, which draws to you everything good that you desire.

⊹ 323 ⊹

Your pure, almost childlike, faith has drawn the help of powerful and loving ascended masters who are by your side at this moment. They are ready to help you with your prayers.

⁙ 324 ⁙

You stand shoulder to shoulder with benevolent guardian angels, archangels, and ascended masters. Surrounded by such powerful Divine love, you can feel certain of a positive outcome to this situation.

⁙ 325 ⁙

The changes that you're making or considering have been guided by the wise and loving ascended masters. You can walk along the path of healthy change with certainty that you're doing the right thing.

⁙ 326 ⁙

Give any fears or concerns regarding your material needs to the ascended masters, and they'll increase your faith to help supply your needs.

⁙ 327 ⁙

The ascended masters are applauding the path you're on. The more you trust the validity of your intuitive guidance upon this path, the better everything goes.

⊹ 328 ⊹

Your faith, and prayers to the ascended masters, have helped you experience an increase in abundance (such as time, money, and other areas of your life).

⊹ 329 ⊹

Trust that the ascended masters are helping you with your Divine life purpose, because they are.

⊹ 330 ⊹

You and your life are filled with the love of God and the ascended masters. Open your heart to receive this love, and be nourished now.

⊹ 331 ⊹

The ascended masters remind you that their lives were testaments to the power of positive thinking. Keep your words—spoken, written, and thought—on a positive level to attract a more desirable outcome.

⁕ 332 ⁕

Trust that this situation is being healed and handled by the ascended masters, who have heard and answered your prayers.

⁕ 333 ⁕

You are completely surrounded, protected, loved, and guided by the benevolent ascended masters.

⁕ 334 ⁕

Your spiritual connection with the angels, archangels, and ascended masters is clear and very real.

⁕ 335 ⁕

The ascended masters are guiding and protecting you through some necessary and healthy life changes.

⁕ 336 ⁕

Your prayers for help with material needs (such as paying the bills, money for food and shelter, and so forth) have been heard and answered by the ascended masters.

·:· 337 ·:·

You are surrounded by ascended masters who assure you that you are correctly hearing them and following their guidance perfectly.

·:· 338 ·:·

Open your arms to receive all of the gifts the ascended masters are sending you. It is safe for you to receive!

·:· 339 ·:·

You and your Divine life purpose are fully supported by the ascended masters. Ask them for help with any aspect of your career or spiritual path.

·:· 340 ·:·

All of Heaven is watching over you and answering your prayers.

·:· 341 ·:·

You're feeling better now, thanks to the help of the angels, archangels, and ascended masters who are watching over you and your loved ones.

⬧ 342 ⬧

Your prayers have increased your faith, and your connection with the angels and ascended masters. All of these factors help you in every area of your life.

⬧ 343 ⬧

Your spiritual devotion and practices have attracted the help and guidance of many trustworthy angels, archangels, and ascended masters.

⬧ 344 ⬧

You love, and are loved by, the angels and ascended masters. You are very closely connected.

⬧ 345 ⬧

Heaven is helping you make some much-needed and positive life changes.

⬧ 346 ⬧

Your prayers about your material needs have been heard and answered by the angels, archangels, and ascended masters.

⁘ 347 ⁘

Your clear connection with the angels, archangels, and ascended masters has resulted in your receiving and following very accurate Divine guidance. Congratulations, and keep going!

⁘ 348 ⁘

The angels and ascended masters are helping you tap into the Universal flow of abundance. Open your arms and receive!

⁘ 349 ⁘

You and your Divine life purpose are being helped and supported by the angels, archangels, and ascended masters.

⁘ 350 ⁘

The changes that you're experiencing are Divinely guided and will bring blessings to everyone involved.

⁘ 351 ⁘

Know that you are fully supported as you change your life to match your highest visions.

⁘ 352 ⁘

Faithfully walk in the direction of your dreams, trusting that you are Divinely guided through each step.

⁘ 353 ⁘

Ascended masters stand all around you, protecting and supporting you as you alter your life in healthier ways.

⁘ 354 ⁘

Heaven is helping you change your life for the better.

⁘ 355 ⁘

Big, positive changes are imminent in your life, thanks to your prayers and the help of loving ascended masters.

⁘ 356 ⁘

Because you're following your Divine guidance, your life is becoming easier to manage. The worst is now behind you.

⁙ 357 ⁙

Well done! You've been listening to your intuition, and now you're on the right path—changing your life in wonderful ways.

⁙ 358 ⁙

The ascended masters are giving you strong guidance to make beneficial changes in your career and financial life. Listen to and follow your intuition in these life areas to reap these rewards.

⁙ 359 ⁙

The changes that you're making or considering are answers to your prayers about your Divine life purpose. The ascended masters' guidance is accurate and trustworthy.

⁙ 360 ⁙

Heaven is helping you meet your needs and is providing for you. Give any worries or concerns to God and the ascended masters.

❖ 361 ❖

Your prayers about paying your bills and other earthly concerns have been heard and answered. Turn any worries into prayers for help.

❖ 362 ❖

Trust that you're being assisted by powerful and loving ascended masters. They are helping to provide for you and your family.

❖ 363 ❖

The answers to your prayers are materializing into form!

❖ 364 ❖

You are surrounded by angels, archangels, and ascended masters who are supporting you and your family.

❖ 365 ❖

Listen to and follow your intuition, as it is accurately guiding you toward making positive life changes that will improve your health, finances, or other important life areas.

⁘ 366 ⁘

Spiritualize your thinking so that your focus is on love. The more loving you are toward yourself and others, the better everything goes for you.

⁘ 367 ⁘

You're on the right path by following your intuition, which is giving you information that will answer your prayers.

⁘ 368 ⁘

Keep praying, meditating, and following Heaven's guidance, as it is helping you improve your finances and other life areas.

⁘ 369 ⁘

Your prayers about being fully supported on your spiritual path have been heard and answered, and you are fulfilling your Divine life purpose.

⁜ 370 ⁜

You are working in perfect partnership with God and the ascended masters. Continue to listen to and follow your inner guidance, as this is the best path for you to take.

⁜ 371 ⁜

Your prayerful connection to the ascended masters has helped you to hear and follow accurate Divine guidance. Keep going!

⁜ 372 ⁜

Trust that you are on the right path, because you are.

⁜ 373 ⁜

You are moving in the right direction, and are accompanied by powerful and loving ascended masters.

⁜ 374 ⁜

Heaven is applauding the recent choices and actions that you've made! Keep going.

⁙ 375 ⁙

Congratulations for making healthy choices, which truly are answers to your prayers.

⁙ 376 ⁙

The ascended masters are giving you trustworthy guidance on how to improve your life. Listen to this wisdom, which comes to you through your feelings, thoughts, ideas, and other intuitive means.

⁙ 377 ⁙

Well done! You've consulted with Heavenly deities, and are accurately following your Divine guidance.

⁙ 378 ⁙

The ascended masters say that you're on the right course for increasing your abundance.

⁙ 379 ⁙

Keep praying and listening for guidance about your career path, because you are presently on the right track for your Divine life purpose.

⁘ 380 ⁘

God and the ascended masters are watching over you, and fully supporting you in all ways.

⁘ 381 ⁘

The ascended masters urge you to use positive words to describe your finances whenever you speak, think, or write.

⁘ 382 ⁘

Keep the faith that things are improving in your life, especially financially. Your faith can move mountains!

⁘ 383 ⁘

Give any cares about money or other earthly needs to Heaven, as you are lovingly supported and cared for.

⁘ 384 ⁘

Your prayers about finances have been heard and answered by the angels and ascended masters.

⁑ 385 ⁑

The changes that you're making or considering are Divinely guided ways to increase your income.

⁑ 386 ⁑

Give any cares or concerns about finances to the ascended masters, as they're ready to support you in all ways.

⁑ 387 ⁑

Because you are praying and then listening to the Divine answers, you're on the right path, and the flow of Universal abundance has opened to you!

⁑ 388 ⁑

Your prayerful connection with the ascended masters has helped to open you to the flow of Universal abundance, including having plenty of time, money, love, health, and everything that you desire.

❖ 389 ❖

You are fully supported, financially and otherwise, as you follow your heart's desires about career choices.

❖ 390 ❖

God's Divine light and love are shining upon you, helping to support and guide you toward a meaningful career.

❖ 391 ❖

The ascended masters are asking you to keep positive thoughts about your career and Divine purpose. Your thoughts are determining your outcome.

❖ 392 ❖

Trust that you are ready and qualified to work on your Divine life purpose . . . now.

❖ 393 ❖

The ascended masters have heard and answered your prayers about creating more meaning in

your career and in your life. Follow your inner
guidance to find your truth.

⁘ 394 ⁘

You and your Divine purpose are fully supported
by the angels, archangels, and ascended masters.

⁘ 395 ⁘

Your inner guidance is accurately guiding you to
make important life changes that will put you on
the path of your Divine life mission.

⁘ 396 ⁘

Give any cares or concerns about the meaning of
your life to the ascended masters, who hear and
answer your prayers.

⁘ 397 ⁘

You're on the right path toward your Divine life
purpose.

⁘ 398 ⁘

You're being provided for in all ways, as long as you focus your time and energy on your Divine mission in life.

⁘ 399 ⁘

Your Divine life purpose is needed right now, and the ascended masters urge you to get to work on your mission without delay. Ask the ascended masters for any information, courage, or support you may need for your purpose.

⁘ 400 ⁘

God and the angels are surrounding you with love, bliss, and protection.

⁘ 401 ⁘

This is a message from God and the angels, reminding you to stay positive and only focus on your desires and not your fears.

·:· 402 ·:·

God and the angels are helping to increase your faith, which is the magic ingredient in Divine manifestation.

·:· 403 ·:·

God, the angels, and the ascended masters are all rallying around you, giving you extra love and support right now. Call upon them to help you with this current situation, and follow any guidance you receive, as it is an answer to your prayers.

·:· 404 ·:·

You've made God and the angels the center of your consciousness, which has brought you peace and everything else you could desire. Ask them for help with whatever you'd like.

·:· 405 ·:·

God and the angels are helping you change your life for the better.

⸬ 406 ⸬

Your prayers for help with earthly support (such as food, money to pay bills, home, and so on) have been heard and answered. Give any worries to God and the angels.

⸬ 407 ⸬

Heaven is giving you a strong sign that you're heading in a positive direction. Keep going!

⸬ 408 ⸬

God and the angels are helping to answer your prayers about finances. Open your arms to receive their help, which may come in the form of intuitive thoughts, ideas, or people offering assistance.

⸬ 409 ⸬

You are being Divinely supported and guided as to how to improve your career so that it is spiritually and emotionally meaningful.

⋅ 410 ⋅

Your positive affirmations and visualizations are helping you co-create the answers to your prayers. Stay positive, because it's working!

⋅ 411 ⋅

The angels are with you, ready to give you information and guidance. All you need to do is ask.

⋅ 412 ⋅

This is a strong message from the angels, saying that your prayers have been heard. For these prayers to be answered, you'll need to keep a positive mind-set. Ask the angels to help you with this.

⋅ 413 ⋅

There's nothing to fear, as you are supported and lovingly surrounded by angels, archangels, and ascended masters.

⁜ 414 ⁜

The angels are sending you Divinely guided ideas. Trust in their validity, and act upon the ideas that stimulate your interests.

⁜ 415 ⁜

The angels are helping you make positive life changes, and they ask you to relax and trust the process.

⁜ 416 ⁜

Your prayers to improve conditions in your life have been heard and answered by the angels. Stay positive in order to manifest these positive outcomes more rapidly.

⁜ 417 ⁜

The angels want you to know that all of your positive affirmations, visualizations, and prayers have put you on the fast track to the realization of your dreams!

⁝ 418 ⁝

Keep up the good work, as your optimistic outlook and connection to the angels have opened the gateway to financial abundance.

⁝ 419 ⁝

You and your angels are working together on the fruition of your Divine life purpose. Stay in prayerful contact and communication with the angels so you'll always know the best step to take next.

⁝ 420 ⁝

Your prayers, faith, and open heart have created a clear connection between you and the Divine. You're being lovingly helped by God and the angels right now.

⁝ 421 ⁝

The angels say: "Hold a strong and steady positive vision of what you desire; and give us any fears, cares, or worries. Your positive thoughts and faith are creating favorable outcomes for this situation."

⁘ 422 ⁘

This is a strong message from the angels, asking you to trust, believe, and have faith that your prayers are being answered, because they are.

⁘ 423 ⁘

Trust that Heaven is supporting and helping you right now.

⁘ 424 ⁘

The angels are helping to strengthen your faith because they know that a positive outlook will improve the outcome of this situation.

⁘ 425 ⁘

You're hearing your angels correctly as you consider making a healthy life change. Ask them to help you move forward with your plans.

⁘ 426 ⁘

Prayer and positive intentions will help your material needs materialize, while worry only compounds the issues. Ask the angels to boost your faith.

∴ 427 ∴

The angels congratulate you for "keeping the faith," as you are on the right path.

∴ 428 ∴

Your faith and connection to the angels have opened the doors to financial security.

∴ 429 ∴

The angels are working diligently behind the scenes to support you and your life purpose. The doors are open for you; walk through them confidently.

∴ 430 ∴

Your prayers have been heard and answered by all the spiritual beings in Heaven, who are working on your behalf right now.

⁘ 431 ⁘

The more positive your thoughts are, the more easily you can hear the loving and supportive guidance of the angels and ascended masters.

⁘ 432 ⁘

Trust that you're accurately hearing trustworthy Divine guidance from your angels and the ascended masters. This guidance may come in the form of feelings, ideas, visions, or signs.

⁘ 433 ⁘

You are completely surrounded, loved, and supported by the angels and many beloved deities.

⁘ 434 ⁘

Give any worries or concerns to the angels and ascended masters, who are embracing you right this minute with healing love.

❖ 435 ❖

Congratulations on listening to your inner wisdom and making healthy life changes. Your healthy choices are answers to your prayers.

❖ 436 ❖

The angels and ascended masters have heard and answered your prayers, and your physical needs are being met.

❖ 437 ❖

You are following your Divine guidance accurately, and as a result, you're on the right pathway.

❖ 438 ❖

The angels and ascended masters say that they're helping your financial needs to be met.

❖ 439 ❖

Have conversations with your guides and angels about your Divine life purpose, and follow their guidance without delay.

⁙ 440 ⁙

God and the angels love you very much, and are helping you through this situation.

⁙ 441 ⁙

The angels and archangels say that your thoughts are manifesting rapidly into material form, so be sure to only think about your desires. Ask the angels for help in staying positive.

⁙ 442 ⁙

The angels and archangels are urging you to stay positive, as your optimism supports them in answering your prayers.

⁙ 443 ⁙

You are completely protected and loved by the ascended masters and angels, who have heard your prayers and are answering your call for help.

⁙ 444 ⁙

There are angels—they're everywhere around you! You are completely loved, supported, and guided by many Heavenly beings, and you have nothing to fear.

⁘ 445 ⁘

The angels are fully supporting you through the changes that you're currently making or considering. Go ahead with your plans.

⁘ 446 ⁘

The angels are helping you with your material needs for shelter, food, finances, and so forth.

⁘ 447 ⁘

The angels are congratulating and encouraging you, because you're on the right path for the full manifestation of all of your dreams!

⁘ 448 ⁘

The angels and archangels are helping you with finances, so be sure to notice and follow any intuitive thoughts that inspire you to take positive action, as this is one way that the angels are helping you. Expect financial improvements, as they're on their way.

⁛ 449 ⁛

The angels and mighty archangels are supporting your life purpose and spiritually based work. Move forward confidently in the direction of your career dreams.

⁛ 450 ⁛

God and the angels are supporting you through your life changes. Give any fears or worries to them.

⁛ 451 ⁛

The angels say that the changes you're making are good ones, and all that is needed on your part is a positive outlook.

⁛ 452 ⁛

The angels are boosting your faith and confidence about the changes you're making or considering.

⁛ 453 ⁛

Go ahead and make the changes that you're considering, as you are completely protected and supported by the angels and ascended masters.

⁘ 454 ⁘

The changes that you're considering have been suggested to you by your guardian angels and the archangels. You are literally answering your prayers as you take these necessary steps to make healthful changes.

⁘ 455 ⁘

Please don't worry about the big and sudden changes occurring in your life right now, as they were nudged along by the angels, who were answering your prayers. The angels are supporting you as you change your life in blessed ways.

⁘ 456 ⁘

Give any worries or concerns about the changes you're currently making or considering to the angels. These changes are bringing great blessings into your life.

⁘ 457 ⁘

You're on the right path as far as the changes you're making in your life, and the angels are with you every step of the way.

⁙ 458 ⁙

Trust the changes you're being guided to make, as your positive actions today are investments in your future.

⁙ 459 ⁙

The angels have guided you to make positive life changes that will put you on the path of your Divine life purpose.

⁙ 460 ⁙

God and the angels are taking care of your earthly needs. Keep your heart and mind centered on spiritual love, and let Heaven do the rest.

⁙ 461 ⁙

You and the angels are co-creating the answers to your prayers. Your role is to keep your thoughts as positive as possible. Ask the angels for help with this, too.

⁙ 462 ⁙

The angels ask you to "keep the faith" about your prayers being answered. The angels are working behind the scenes to help you, as you'll soon see.

⁙ 463 ⁙

You've attracted major help with your prayers! You have ascended masters, guardian angels, and the archangels working on answering your prayers.

⁙ 464 ⁙

The angels are surrounding you with their Divine protection, love, and support in all ways.

⁙ 465 ⁙

Follow the intuitive guidance that you've been receiving about making healthy changes in your life. These changes will bring the answers to your prayers that you've been seeking.

⁙ 466 ⁙

Give any earthly concerns (such as finances, career, relationship, home, and so forth) to the angels. Turn every worry into a prayer for help, and you'll soon see and feel the light in your life.

⁘ 467 ⁘

The angels say that you're on the right path, and are reaping benefits in spiritual and material ways. Keep going.

⁘ 468 ⁘

Your prayers for help with your finances have been heard and answered by the angels, who ask you to give any worries or concerns to them. All is well.

⁘ 469 ⁘

The angels are helping you pay the bills and have food and shelter, while you focus on your Divine life purpose.

⁘ 470 ⁘

Your spiritual devotion and practices have put you on a very healthy pathway. You're exactly where you need to be right now.

⋇ 471 ⋇

The more you use positive words in your thoughts, speech, and writing, the better you'll feel.

⋇ 472 ⋇

The angels ask you to trust that everything is in Divine and perfect order, because it is.

⋇ 473 ⋇

You and your loved ones are held in the hands of loving angels and ascended masters, who are completely supporting you in all ways. Give them any worries or cares.

⋇ 474 ⋇

The angels applaud you for making good choices for yourself, and they encourage you to keep going along your healthy pathway.

⋇ 475 ⋇

The changes that you're making or considering are moving your life in a very positive direction.

The angels are overseeing these changes to ensure that they're gentle and healing.

⁙ 476 ⁙

The angels want you to know that they've heard and answered your prayers about paying your bills and other concerns. All is well.

⁙ 477 ⁙

You've accurately listened to your angels, and as a result of following your Divine guidance, you're taking steps toward the realization of your heart's dreams.

⁙ 478 ⁙

The angels say that you're on the right path as far as improving your finances.

⁙ 479 ⁙

The thoughts, ideas, and actions that relate to your career and life purpose are Divinely guided by the angels.

❖ 480 ❖

Open your arms to receive the abundance of good that Heaven is giving you. Notice the gifts that come to you throughout the day.

❖ 481 ❖

The angels are helping you stay optimistic and positive about your money situation, and as a result, abundance is coming to you.

❖ 482 ❖

Trust that the angels are supporting you in all ways, because they are.

❖ 483 ❖

Your prayers for financial help have been heard and answered by the angels, archangels, and ascended masters.

❖ 484 ❖

You are completely surrounded by loving and supportive angels who are helping you with every area of your life, especially career and finances.

⊹ 485 ⊹

The angels are helping you change, improve, and heal your career and financial life so that you're in line with your highest good.

⊹ 486 ⊹

The angels are reassuring you that they're helping you pay your bills and meet all material needs for you and your loved ones. Give any worries or cares to the angels, and know that all is well.

⊹ 487 ⊹

You are accurately hearing and following your angels' guidance about your career and finances, and as a result, you're on the right path for the fruition of your dreams.

⊹ 488 ⊹

The angels are helping you manifest abundance and the answers to your prayers.

⁙ 489 ⁙

Trust that the angels are supporting you as you focus on your spiritually based career and life purpose.

⁙ 490 ⁙

Your career and life purpose are watched over and protected by God and the angels.

⁙ 491 ⁙

The more positive you are about your career, the better everything goes.

⁙ 492 ⁙

Trust that the angels are helping you find a meaningful career.

⁙ 493 ⁙

Your prayers about your Divine life purpose and career have been heard and answered by the angels, archangels, and ascended masters.

⁖ 494 ⁖

Your angels walk beside you, guiding you along every step of your career and Divine life purpose.

⁖ 495 ⁖

The angels are fully supporting you as you change your life so that you can fully focus on your spiritual passions as a career.

⁖ 496 ⁖

The angels assure you that all of your bills will be paid and your needs will be met as you focus on your spiritually satisfying career options.

⁖ 497 ⁖

The angels say that you're doing the right thing by focusing on your Divine life purpose right now.

⁖ 498 ⁖

You and your spiritually based career are supported in all ways by the angels.

⁘ 499 ⁘

The angels urge you to completely focus your time and energy on your spiritually based career and your Divine life purpose.

⁘ 500 ⁘

Your renewed spiritual devotion has connected you to God's infinite wisdom. Follow God's guidance to make healthy changes in your life.

⁘ 501 ⁘

As you make changes, it's important that you keep your thoughts focused on Divine wisdom, which is taking care of every detail. Stay positive and prayerfully connected to God.

⁘ 502 ⁘

Trust that the changes you're making, or are about to make, are Divinely guided by God's infinite love and wisdom.

⁘ 503 ⁘

Heaven is helping you to change and improve your life. Your ideas are inspired by God and the ascended masters, who are watching over and protecting you and your loved ones.

⁘ 504 ⁘

Be aware of, and follow, your feelings or thoughts about making positive changes in your life.

⁘ 505 ⁘

Now that you've put God and spirituality at the center of your life, everything will change for you. Trust and know that these changes are answers to your prayers, and that God is protecting and supporting you.

⁘ 506 ⁘

God is providing for all of your material needs, including improving your home and work life.

⁘ 507 ⁘

God says that you're on the right path with the changes you're making or considering. Move forward with your plans.

⁘ 508 ⁘

Your prayers and life changes have resulted in an increase in financial flow.

⁘ 509 ⁘

The changes that you're experiencing are preparing you for the fulfillment of your Divine life purpose.

⁘ 510 ⁘

Congratulations! Your new spiritual practices have elevated your thoughts and spiritual frequencies. Stay positive, as your thoughts are creating healthy changes in your life.

⁘ 511 ⁘

Replace old habits of negativity with a new and more positive approach.

⬩ 512 ⬩

Keep working on increasing your faith and positive outlook, as it is having a very real and beneficial effect on your life.

⬩ 513 ⬩

The ascended masters and your positive affirmations are transforming your life in wonderful ways.

⬩ 514 ⬩

Give any questions or concerns about changing your life to the angels, and they will help you feel more clear and confident about your next steps.

⬩ 515 ⬩

You've adopted a new, and much more positive, approach to life. This may mean that your relationships and other aspects of your life will change . . . all for the best.

⬦ 516 ⬦

The changes that you're making, combined with your positive approach and attitude, help you to enjoy each day more.

⬦ 517 ⬦

Keep going with your renewed positive outlook and affirmations, as this is making a healthy difference in your life.

⬦ 518 ⬦

Your more spiritualized and optimistic thoughts about money have opened the flow of abundance for you.

⬦ 519 ⬦

Hold positive thoughts about your career. Avoid worrying or complaining about work, as your thoughts are steering the journey of your Divine life purpose.

⁜ 520 ⁜

Trust that Heaven is helping you change your life in positive ways.

⁜ 521 ⁜

As you approach new opportunities and relationships, it's vital that you stay optimistic and use only positive words in your thoughts, speech, and writing.

⁜ 522 ⁜

With faith you can do anything! Truly believe that your prayers to improve your life have been heard and answered.

⁜ 523 ⁜

The ascended masters are guiding you to release the old and embrace the new.

⁜ 524 ⁜

Angels and archangels are watching over your new projects and helping you transform your ideas and dreams into reality.

⁑ 525 ⁑

Trust that the big changes you're experiencing are for the best, and that things will calm down soon.

⁑ 526 ⁑

Have faith that your new methods and approaches are improving your life, including your finances, health, and relationships.

⁑ 527 ⁑

Know that your decision to make positive changes is the right idea. Move forward with these decisions confidently!

⁑ 528 ⁑

Trust that your new ideas will be financially successful, because they will be.

⁑ 529 ⁑

Follow your inner guidance about creating a spiritually meaningful career, which is your Divine life purpose.

⁖ 530 ⁖

God and the ascended masters are counseling you to make healthy life choices and to take good care of yourself.

⁖ 531 ⁖

Stay positive about the changes you're making, or are thinking of making, because the idea to make these changes is Divinely guided.

⁖ 532 ⁖

Trust that the ascended masters are giving you the courage and motivation to improve your life.

⁖ 533 ⁖

Your prayers for guidance on how to change your life have been heard and answered by many ascended masters who love and protect you.

⁖ 534 ⁖

You're completely supported by the angels and ascended masters as you go through some positive and life-changing experiences.

✢ 535 ✢

Keep your entire focus centered upon prayers and spirituality as you venture into new areas in your life.

✢ 536 ✢

The ascended masters say that your changed focus is helping you ease the stress of everyday life.

✢ 537 ✢

The changes that you're making are Divinely guided and a very good idea.

✢ 538 ✢

Your finances are improving, thanks to your prayerful connection to the ascended masters and because you're following their trustworthy guidance.

✢ 539 ✢

The ascended masters say that your life is changing for the better, especially with respect to your Divine life purpose and spiritually meaningful career.

⁙ 540 ⁙

God and the angels are now giving you strong messages to make healthy life changes.

⁙ 541 ⁙

The angels ask you to hold positive thoughts about improving your life, as your thoughts are influencing the outcome.

⁙ 542 ⁙

Trust that the angels are watching over you as you change your life for the better.

⁙ 543 ⁙

Loving and powerful angels, archangels, and ascended masters are answering your prayers, and your life is improving each day.

⁙ 544 ⁙

You are surrounded by loving and supportive angels, who are helping you change your life in beautiful ways.

∴ 545 ∴

Keep in constant prayerful contact with the angels as you venture into new life areas. Give any fears or concerns to them.

∴ 546 ∴

The angels are helping you improve your home and work life.

∴ 547 ∴

Congratulations for talking to your angels, listening to their guidance, and getting yourself on the right path.

∴ 548 ∴

The angels say that the changes you're making will give you more financial security.

∴ 549 ∴

Talk to the angels continually about your Divine life purpose, as they will help you adjust your life so that your work is spiritually centered.

⚜ 550 ⚜

God is watching over you as you experience major life changes.

⚜ 551 ⚜

Keep a positive mind-set about improving your life, because the words that you use in thought, speech, and writing can either help or hinder you.

⚜ 552 ⚜

Trust that your life is getting better, because it is.

⚜ 553 ⚜

It's time to make healthy changes in your life, and you are supported through these changes by the ascended masters.

⚜ 554 ⚜

The angels reassure you that the changes you're experiencing are bringing you blessings. Let the old go, and welcome the new.

⁘ 555 ⁘

Huge changes are rumbling throughout your entire life! To keep these changes on the highest possible course, be sure to keep your thoughts positive, and stay centered in prayer and affirmations.

⁘ 556 ⁘

Follow through on your new ideas and opportunities, as they will make your life easier and relieve you of stress.

⁘ 557 ⁘

The changes that you're making or considering are exactly right for you at this time.

⁘ 558 ⁘

You're investing in *you* with your recent activities. Now that you're taking better care of yourself, you'll soon see the rewards flowing to you.

⁘ 559 ⁘

It's time to change your career focus so that it's more meaningful and aligned with your spiritual beliefs.

⁘ 560 ⁘

Turn to God for help with your life stressors, and make changes that are in Divine alignment with your intuition.

⁘ 561 ⁘

Your new positive outlook with respect to your home and work life is changing everything for the better.

⁘ 562 ⁘

Trust that you can improve in all areas, including your finances, home life, and career. Your faith opens up new doors of opportunity.

⁘ 563 ⁘

Give any cares or worries to the ascended masters, and follow their Divine guidance, which comes to you as intuition or ideas.

⁘ 564 ⁘

The angels are helping you improve your life so that things are easier for you at home and work.

∴ 565 ∴

The circumstances in your life are forcing you to make changes that will ultimately bring great blessings to you and your loved ones.

∴ 566 ∴

See yourself as strong and powerful. Take charge of improving your life.

∴ 567 ∴

The changes that you're making or considering are good ideas and will help you ease the stress in your life.

∴ 568 ∴

The flow of Universal abundance is open to you, as long as you stay true to yourself by following your intuition—especially when it urges you to make healthy changes.

⁙ 569 ⁙

The more you focus on possibilities and prayers, the more confident and supported you'll feel about your Divine life purpose.

⁙ 570 ⁙

You're following God's wisdom in your decision to make healthy life changes.

⁙ 571 ⁙

Stay positive about the improvements you're making, as they're the right thing to do.

⁙ 572 ⁙

Trust that your life is getting better, because it is.

⁙ 573 ⁙

You're accurately following Divine guidance from the ascended masters, and making remarkable strides and progress.

⁘ 574 ⁘

The angels are helping you take steps that greatly improve your life.

⁘ 575 ⁘

The big changes that you're experiencing are answers to your prayers, and bring blessings to you and your loved ones.

⁘ 576 ⁘

Give any fear or doubts about changing your life to Heaven, as these changes will ease a lot of stress.

⁘ 577 ⁘

Well done! You're taking the right steps and are on the right path.

⁘ 578 ⁘

Your idea is clear and right on the mark, and it will improve your financial life.

⁙ 579 ⁙

It's time to change your career so that it is more meaningful and fulfilling.

⁙ 580 ⁙

Keep your focus on God and spirituality, and all of your earthly needs will be Divinely taken care of.

⁙ 581 ⁙

Your new positive mind-set as well as the affirmations you're stating or thinking are changing your finances for the better.

⁙ 582 ⁙

Trust that your financial needs are being met, as your faith evokes positive manifestation.

⁙ 583 ⁙

The ascended masters have heard and answered your prayers about relieving financial stress, and they're guiding you to make healthy changes that will improve your situation. Follow your intuition and make the changes accordingly.

❖ 584 ❖

Give any worries or cares, especially about career or finances, to the angels, as they will help you find your way to the Universal support that is available to all.

❖ 585 ❖

To improve your finances, you'll need to make some major life changes. You already know what some of these changes are, so take steps in that direction . . . today!

❖ 586 ❖

You'll find relief from financial stress through prayer, affirmations, and spending time working on projects that you find meaningful.

❖ 587 ❖

Your new business venture is putting you on the path to success.

❖ 588 ❖

Your recent changes have helped you to adopt healthy new financial habits, which have opened the flow of abundance for you.

❖ 589 ❖

As you change your career so that it is more satisfying and fulfilling, your financial needs are being met.

❖ 590 ❖

Put your focus entirely on the question, "How may I be of spiritual service?" and let God take care of all the other details. All you need to do is listen for the voice of love, and follow its gentle guidance, which may ask you to make healthy changes.

❖ 591 ❖

As you hold positive thoughts about your Divine purpose, your career becomes more meaningful and spiritually oriented.

❖ 592 ❖

Trust that you are fully supported as you devote your time and energy to developing your spiritually based career.

❖ 593 ❖

The ascended masters have heard and answered your prayers about improving your career so that it is more meaningful and fulfilling for you.

❖ 594 ❖

The angels are helping you make healthy and much-needed changes that allow you to devote your time to your Divine purpose.

❖ 595 ❖

Change your career so that it is more spiritually centered.

❖ 596 ❖

As you focus on serving a spiritual purpose in your career, all of life's details become easier to manage.

⸪ 597 ⸪

You're on the right path with your ideas and actions concerning your career.

⸪ 598 ⸪

Your new spiritually based business venture will be very successful.

⸪ 599 ⸪

This message urges you to change your thoughts and actions so that your time is completely devoted to fulfilling your Divine life purpose (which involves an issue that is near and dear to your heart).

⸪ 600 ⸪

Give any worries or stress to God, who is watching over and supporting you.

⸪ 601 ⸪

Your prayers, positive thinking, and focus on God help you alleviate the stress in your life.

⁛ 602 ⁛

Trust that God is helping you with your daily needs, because this is true.

⁛ 603 ⁛

Your prayers for help have been heard and answered by God and the ascended masters (such as Jesus and the saints).

⁛ 604 ⁛

God and the angels are watching over you and your loved ones, ensuring that you're protected and provided for.

⁛ 605 ⁛

God is helping you improve your life so that you have more peace of mind.

⁛ 606 ⁛

As you put God and spirituality at the center of your life, everything else takes care of itself.

⊹ 607 ⊹

Your spiritual focus has put you on the right path, and your needs are being taken care of.

⊹ 608 ⊹

Give any worries about money to God, who is providing for all of your needs.

⊹ 609 ⊹

Talk to God about your Divine life purpose, including any questions or concerns about your career and spiritual path.

⊹ 610 ⊹

Use positive affirmations and prayer for relief from stress.

⊹ 611 ⊹

The words that you think, speak, and write are determining how things go for you, so focus on your desires and positive outcomes.

⸪ 612 ⸪

Stay positive about this situation, as your optimism and faith will create a better outcome.

⸪ 613 ⸪

The ascended masters are helping you feel happy and peaceful regarding this situation.

⸪ 614 ⸪

Give any stress or worries to the angels, who are helping you with your everyday concerns.

⸪ 615 ⸪

Your new positive outlook is improving your home and work life.

⸪ 616 ⸪

Look only at possibilities and not at material illusions. You are powerful and can overcome any situation using a positive mind-set.

⁘ 617 ⁘

Keep going with your new spiritual approach, because it is having positive effects upon you and your life.

⁘ 618 ⁘

Your manifestation practices are working. Keep visualizing and affirming abundance.

⁘ 619 ⁘

Stay positive about your career and finances, and put your entire focus on serving a spiritual purpose through your work.

⁘ 620 ⁘

Trust that God is taking care of your needs, because this is true.

⁘ 621 ⁘

Faith and positive thoughts are resolving this situation beautifully, so continue with this healthy practice.

⁂ 622 ⁂

This is a strong message from the angels urging you to "keep the faith" that everything will be okay, because it will.

⁂ 623 ⁂

Trust that the ascended masters have heard and answered your prayers for help, because they have.

⁂ 624 ⁂

Have faith in the angels' miraculous abilities to help and support you.

⁂ 625 ⁂

Trust that the changes you're making or considering will help improve this situation.

⁂ 626 ⁂

No matter what is going on around you, keep the faith that it will all work out. Your faith makes a positive difference in the outcome.

⁘ 627 ⁘

Your faith is warranted because your current activities are vastly improving your home and work life.

⁘ 628 ⁘

Trust that you will always have enough money to cover your expenses and support yourself.

⁘ 629 ⁘

Have faith that you'll be able to support yourself as you devote yourself to your Divine life purpose.

⁘ 630 ⁘

Give any worries to God and the ascended masters, and ask for their help with this situation so that they can intervene.

⁘ 631 ⁘

The ascended masters ask you to stay positive about this situation, as your thoughts are influencing the outcome.

∴ 632 ∴

Trust that the ascended masters have heard and answered your prayers, because they have.

∴ 633 ∴

You have nothing to worry about, because the ascended masters are taking care of this situation.

∴ 634 ∴

Give any worries or cares to the angels and ascended masters, who are with you right now.

∴ 635 ∴

The ascended masters are helping you improve your life, so know that the changes you're experiencing are blessings.

∴ 636 ∴

Allow the ascended masters to relieve you of stress through prayer and meditation.

⁙ 637 ⁙

Everything related to this situation is beautifully resolved!

⁙ 638 ⁙

The ascended masters have heard and answered your prayers about your career and finances.

⁙ 639 ⁙

Your Divine life purpose is watched over and helped by the ascended masters, who support you in all ways through your spiritually based career.

⁙ 640 ⁙

Give any worries to God and the angels, who love you unconditionally and want to help you with this situation. You are not alone!

⁙ 641 ⁙

The angels ask you to trade worries for prayer, as worries attract more of the same, but prayers attract miracles.

⁙ 642 ⁙

Trust that the angels are taking care of this situation, because they are.

⁙ 643 ⁙

Heaven is helping you overcome a stressful experience by sending angels and archangels to your side. Ask them for help with any aspect of this situation, and be open to their help and guidance.

⁙ 644 ⁙

You have nothing to worry about, because there are many angels with you right at this moment. Give any fears to them.

⁙ 645 ⁙

The angels are by your side every step of the way as you embark upon new chapters in your life.

⁙ 646 ⁙

The only thing blocking you is worry, and fortunately, the angels will relieve you of this stress if you ask for their help.

⁘ 647 ⁘

The angels have heard your call for help, and they're reassuring you that everything is taken care of.

⁘ 648 ⁘

Give any money worries to the angels, who are ensuring that all of your needs are met.

⁘ 649 ⁘

The angels are supporting you and your Divine life purpose in all ways.

⁘ 650 ⁘

God is helping you through the changes you're experiencing, and everything is working out for your highest good.

⁘ 651 ⁘

The more you keep a positive mind-set, the better the changes you're currently experiencing will work out.

⁘ 652 ⁘

Trust that everything is happening exactly as it's supposed to, because it is. Have faith that all is well.

⁘ 653 ⁘

The ascended masters have heard and answered your prayers about improving your life. They're reassuring you that everything is taken care of. You just need to listen for and follow your intuitive guidance.

⁘ 654 ⁘

The angels are supporting you as you take steps to improve your life.

⁘ 655 ⁘

The big changes that you're going through will bring great blessings into your life, and will ultimately mean that your life gets easier.

⁘ 656 ⁘

All is well, even though appearances might feel stressful. Beneath it all, there is Divine order. You will soon see that the changes that are occurring are answers to your prayers.

⁙ 657 ⁙

This situation can go either way, depending on whether your focus is positive or fear based. Ask the angels to lift your thoughts and outlook so that you can attract the best possible outcome.

⁙ 658 ⁙

Trust that the changes you're experiencing are answers to your prayers about your career and finances.

⁙ 659 ⁙

Call upon the angels to help you make changes that will allow you more time and energy to devote to your spiritual calling and Divine life purpose.

⁙ 660 ⁙

Give any and all worries or concerns to God, who can help you with every detail.

∴ 661 ∴

The best approach to this situation is positive affirmations, and focusing your thoughts on your desires.

∴ 662 ∴

Trust that all is well, because it is.

∴ 663 ∴

Call upon the ascended masters to help you with this situation. Because of free will, they can only help you with your permission (such as through a request, an affirmation, or a prayer).

∴ 664 ∴

The angels are helping you exchange fears and negative thinking for peace and positivity, in answer to your prayers for help.

∴ 665 ∴

To transform this situation and improve your life, it's time to make healthy changes right now. Ask the angels for help with this.

⁙ 666 ⁙

Your thoughts are too focused on material illusions. Raise your thoughts spiritually to get your life back on track.

⁙ 667 ⁙

You're on the verge of a huge positive breakthrough that will offer you a lot of the solutions and answers you've been seeking.

⁙ 668 ⁙

Know that God is your Source of all good things, including the money that you need to pay your bills and meet your needs.

⁙ 669 ⁙

There's nothing to fear regarding your Divine life purpose and spiritually based career. All you need to do is ask for Heaven's help, and then listen for and heed the intuition that follows.

⁘ 670 ⁘

God is helping you put your life on course, so continue to follow the light.

⁘ 671 ⁘

This situation is determined by the degree that you use positive words in your thoughts, speech, and writing. The more positive you are, the better the outcome.

⁘ 672 ⁘

Trust that you are exactly where you need to be right now, and that you're learning valuable lessons and gaining strength.

⁘ 673 ⁘

Keep praying and giving concerns to the ascended masters, because your prayers are working.

⁘ 674 ⁘

The angels are with you, saying that you're on the right path, so have no fear.

∴ 675 ∴

You've had enough of feeling stressed or upset, so you've made some very beneficial and healthy changes. The worst is now behind you.

∴ 676 ∴

Have no worries, as you're doing the right thing.

∴ 677 ∴

If you've been wondering whether you're heading in the right direction, this is a message to tell you that you are.

∴ 678 ∴

A huge improvement in your finances is occurring right now.

∴ 679 ∴

You're going in the right direction as far as your career and Divine life purpose are concerned.

⸭ 680 ⸭

God has heard and answered your prayers to be relieved of financial stress so that all of your earthly needs are met.

⸭ 681 ⸭

Stay positive about financial matters, as your thoughts are influencing the outcome of this situation.

⸭ 682 ⸭

Trust that you'll have enough money to pay your bills and fulfill your needs.

⸭ 683 ⸭

The ascended masters have heard and answered your prayers for financial security, so have no fear.

⸭ 684 ⸭

You are fully supported by the angels, who watch over and protect you and your loved ones.

⸭ 685 ⸭

The changes that you're making will ease financial stress.

⸭ 686 ⸭

To improve your financial situation, affirm and visualize abundance.

⸭ 687 ⸭

You've got the right idea, and it will be successful as long as you stay positive.

⸭ 688 ⸭

Your joy and gratitude keep the gates of abundance open for you, so continue to focus on what you have and you will attract even more into your life.

⸭ 689 ⸭

You and your spiritually based career are financially supported.

∴ 690 ∴

God is providing for your earthly needs while you put your focus on being of spiritual service through your work or volunteer activities.

∴ 691 ∴

Stay positive about your career and life purpose, as optimism attracts business success.

∴ 692 ∴

Trust that your bills will be paid as you focus on following your spiritual calling to heal, teach, or otherwise be of service.

∴ 693 ∴

The ascended masters are watching over you and your needs so that you can devote your time and energy to your Divine mission.

∴ 694 ∴

The angels have heard and answered your prayers about developing your spiritual practice and purpose. The angels are supporting you and your career in all ways.

⁘ 695 ⁘

Keep a steady and unwavering focus on your spiritual guidance and purpose, as it will support you.

⁘ 696 ⁘

Put your focus on following your spiritual calling, and your material needs will be met.

⁘ 697 ⁘

You're on the right path with your ideas and actions concerning your career, so have no worries or fears.

⁘ 698 ⁘

You're on the verge of a career breakthrough that will help you feel financially secure.

⁘ 699 ⁘

Put any worries behind you, and take daily action in the direction of your spiritual calling.

⁑ 700 ⁑

Keep following your Divine guidance, as you have a very clear connection with God, and as a result, you're on the right path.

⁑ 701 ⁑

Your prayers and positive affirmations have pointed you in the right direction.

⁑ 702 ⁑

Trust that you are exactly where you need to be, doing exactly what you need to do.

⁑ 703 ⁑

God and the ascended masters are encouraging you to keep going, because you're on the right path.

⁑ 704 ⁑

The steps that you're currently taking are watched over and protected by God and the angels.

∻ 705 ∻

Now is the perfect time for you to make healthy life changes, as you are protected by God's love and strength.

∻ 706 ∻

You're headed in the right direction in your life, especially the financial and home areas.

∻ 707 ∻

God's wisdom is guiding you in the right way. Move forward with confidence.

∻ 708 ∻

You are fully supported, in financial and other ways, in following your dreams.

∻ 709 ∻

This is the perfect point to focus your time and energy on your Divine life purpose, which is a career path that expresses your heart's desire to heal, help, and be of service.

⁖ 710 ⁖

Your prayers and positive thoughts have steered you in the right direction.

⁖ 711 ⁖

Continue with your affirmations and visualizations, as they're working!

⁖ 712 ⁖

Trust that all of your manifestation efforts are turning your dreams into reality.

⁖ 713 ⁖

The ascended masters, especially the goddesses, are congratulating you for your choices and actions. Keep up the good work!

⁖ 714 ⁖

Your prayers and connection to the angels have set you upon a wonderful path that will serve you and your loved ones well.

⁂ 715 ⁂

The changes that you're making or considering are exactly the right steps for you to take.

⁂ 716 ⁂

Your positive affirmations have set you on a path that will make it easier for you to meet your material needs.

⁂ 717 ⁂

Your inner vision and heart's desires are right on course. Confidently move forward with your plans.

⁂ 718 ⁂

Your visualizations and affirmations are bringing an abundance of money your way.

⁂ 719 ⁂

You're on the right path for a spiritually based career, as long as you keep your thoughts positive.

⁘ 720 ⁘

Have faith in God and yourself, and know that you are doing the right thing.

⁘ 721 ⁘

Your faith and positive thinking have attracted wonderful and trustworthy new opportunities and relationships.

⁘ 722 ⁘

Your pure faith and optimism have created and attracted miracles.

⁘ 723 ⁘

Trust that the ascended masters are with you, guiding and supporting you.

⁘ 724 ⁘

The angels ask you to trust and "keep the faith," because everything about this situation is resolving and healing.

⁙ 725 ⁙

Have faith in the ideas and thoughts you have about making changes, because they are Divinely inspired.

⁙ 726 ⁙

Faith, not worry, is what manifests your desires. Trust, trust, trust.

⁙ 727 ⁙

Your pure faith is attracting every good thing, person, and opportunity to you.

⁙ 728 ⁙

Trust that your finances are improving, because they are.

⁙ 729 ⁙

Believe in yourself and your ability to make a positive difference in this world. Take action, knowing that you're safe and supported as you focus on your Divine life purpose.

⋅⊹⋅ 730 ⋅⊹⋅

You have a clear connection with God and the ascended masters, and you're accurately listening to and following their Divine guidance.

⋅⊹⋅ 731 ⋅⊹⋅

Continue your daily practice of prayer and meditation, because it keeps you centered in a loving mind-set.

⋅⊹⋅ 732 ⋅⊹⋅

Trust that you are accurately hearing Divine guidance from the ascended masters.

⋅⊹⋅ 733 ⋅⊹⋅

The ascended masters are very pleased that you're following your intuitive Divine guidance, which is the answer to your prayers.

⋅⊹⋅ 734 ⋅⊹⋅

Angels and ascended masters are watching over you, ensuring that everything goes well, especially concerning new ventures and relationships.

⁙ 735 ⁙

You are accurately hearing and following your Divine guidance.

⁙ 736 ⁙

You're doing a good job of releasing fears and worries to the ascended masters so that you fully express your Divine qualities of creativity, wisdom, joy, peace, and love.

⁙ 737 ⁙

The ascended masters say that you're flying high, so keep up the good work.

⁙ 738 ⁙

You've accurately listened to your Divine guidance, which has put you on the path of increased abundance.

⁙ 739 ⁙

The ascended masters are helping and guiding you with your career and your Divine life purpose. Keep praying, meditating, and following your intuitive guidance.

∴ 740 ∴

God and the angels are working closely with you on this situation, reassuring you that you're doing the right thing and that all is well.

∴ 741 ∴

The angels ask you to stay positive about the steps you're taking, because you're going in the right direction.

∴ 742 ∴

Trust that the angels are guiding and protecting you in this situation, because they are.

∴ 743 ∴

The angels and ascended masters have heard and answered your prayers in the form of giving you Divine guidance, which you're accurately listening to and following.

⁘ 744 ⁘

You have a clear connection with the angels, and as a result, you're following very accurate intuitive guidance.

⁘ 745 ⁘

The angels are helping you change your life for the better.

⁘ 746 ⁘

Give any concerns or worries to the angels; and focus on your desires, dreams, and what you're currently grateful for in your life.

⁘ 747 ⁘

The angels are telling you to soar high in the direction of your dreams.

⁘ 748 ⁘

You are supported by the angels in all ways, including the financial area.

⁘ 749 ⁘

The angels say that you're heading in the right direction with your career choices.

⁘ 750 ⁘

The changes that you're making or considering are healthful, beneficial, and Divinely inspired.

⁘ 751 ⁘

The improvements that you make right now are wonderful investments that yield happy dividends for you.

⁘ 752 ⁘

Trust that you're doing the right thing by making positive changes in your life, because you are.

⁘ 753 ⁘

The ascended masters are guiding you to make healthful changes in your life. Follow your intuition accordingly.

∴ 754 ∴

As you change your life for the better, angels walk along side you to protect and guide you.

∴ 755 ∴

You are going through major life changes, which are bringing great blessings into your life.

∴ 756 ∴

It's a good time to try new ideas and ways, as they will improve your life dramatically.

∴ 757 ∴

Yes, it's a good idea to make the move that you're considering.

∴ 758 ∴

Your new thoughts and ideas about money are accurate and trustworthy.

⁖ 759 ⁖

It's the right time to put your focus and energy into creating a spiritually meaningful career that makes your heart sing.

⁖ 760 ⁖

Keep a steady focus on God and spirituality to ensure consistent harmony. Your thoughts are powerful, so only focus on your blessings and desires and give any worries to God.

⁖ 761 ⁖

You'll have enough money to pay your bills and meet your needs, provided that you stay on the path of positive thinking and Divinely guided action.

⁖ 762 ⁖

Trust that your needs are being taken care of, now that you're taking better care of yourself and listening to your intuition.

⁘ 763 ⁘

Give any worries or indecision to the ascended masters, who will guide you along the right path for your home and work life.

⁘ 764 ⁘

The angels are watching over you, ensuring that your earthly needs are met.

⁘ 765 ⁘

The changes that you're making or considering have put you on the right path toward relieving stress and increasing your well-being.

⁘ 766 ⁘

All is well. Your bills will be paid and your needs will be met. Turn any worries into prayers for help.

⁘ 767 ⁘

Although you may not yet see them, the answers to your prayers are here. Don't quit five minutes before the miracle—keep going!

❖ 768 ❖

All of your material needs are, and will be, met as you continue to give any cares or worries to Heaven.

❖ 769 ❖

Everything is working out well for the fruition of your spiritually based career and life purpose.

❖ 770 ❖

God is watching over you and your loved ones. Know that you're safe and protected.

❖ 771 ❖

Your new policy of positive thoughts, words, and affirmations has turned your life in healthy new directions.

❖ 772 ❖

Have faith that you're doing the right thing, because you are.

❖ 773 ❖

Your prayers and meditations have helped you to tap into accurate and trustworthy Divine guidance.

❖ 774 ❖

The angels applaud your recent decisions and actions, and they ask you to keep up the good work.

❖ 775 ❖

You are exactly right to make important and healthful changes in your life at this time.

❖ 776 ❖

You are doing everything right to provide for yourself and your loved ones. Give yourself a pat on the back. Congratulations for a job well done!

❖ 777 ❖

You are definitely on the right path in every area of your life. Stay balanced and spiritually aware so that you can continue moving forward on this illuminated path.

⁛ 778 ⁛

You have the Midas touch, and everything you do right now turns to gold.

⁛ 779 ⁛

You're experiencing important breakthroughs concerning your Divine life purpose, so keep going!

⁛ 780 ⁛

Good for you, as you're listening to God's Divine guidance, particularly relating to your career.

⁛ 781 ⁛

As long as you stay positive minded, your career and finances will go very well.

⁛ 782 ⁛

Trust that your financial situation is working itself out, and that all of your needs will be met.

∴ 783 ∴

The ascended masters have heard and answered your prayers about your finances, and they're helping you with this present situation.

∴ 784 ∴

The angels reassure you that you'll have enough money to meet your needs, and that you're moving in the right direction.

∴ 785 ∴

The changes that you're making are definitely improving your financial situation.

∴ 786 ∴

Your intuition has steered you in the right direction, with resultant blessings in your career and finances. Keep going!

∴ 787 ∴

You're "on a roll," and everything is blossoming for you right now, especially in the areas of career and finances. This is a great time to begin new projects, ask for a promotion, and pursue other new career-related endeavors.

⁘ 788 ⁘

Because you're on the right path, you've opened the door to unlimited abundance and Universal support.

⁘ 789 ⁘

Continue moving in the direction you're going with respect to your career, spiritual path, and Divine mission. You will be fully supported all along the way!

⁘ 790 ⁘

You are accurately following God's Divine guidance concerning your career and life purpose.

⁘ 791 ⁘

Your positive thoughts and affirmations about your Divine life purpose are working, so stay with them.

⁘ 792 ⁘

Trust that you're on the right track with respect to your career and life purpose.

⁘ 793 ⁘

The ascended masters are guiding your spiritually based career. Listen to your intuition and follow ideas that come to you, especially if they are focused upon giving service.

⁘ 794 ⁘

The angels are blessing you and your Divine life purpose, helping you to adjust your career so that it is fulfilling.

⁘ 795 ⁘

The career changes that you're making or considering are perfect. These changes will put you in alignment with your soul's purpose, so carry through with them.

⸭ 796 ⸭

You are on the right path for a meaningful career that fully supports you in all ways.

⸭ 797 ⸭

This is a perfect time to start new business ventures and follow through with new career ideas, as you've got the Midas touch right now and everything is golden.

⸭ 798 ⸭

The Universe financially supports you, as you focus on giving service and following the passion of your spiritually based career.

⸭ 799 ⸭

Put your entire focus on providing a service that is aligned with your strong interests and passions, as this is your spiritual purpose, and this service is needed right now.

⁜ 800 ⁜

Give any financial fears to God, who is ensuring that all of your earthly needs are met. You are supported in all ways.

⁜ 801 ⁜

Your prayers and positive thoughts about your finances are keeping you in the flow of abundance.

⁜ 802 ⁜

Keep the faith that God is providing for all of your needs, including helping you with your bills. Follow any Divine intuition that you receive.

⁜ 803 ⁜

Your prayers for help with your finances have been heard and answered.

⁜ 804 ⁜

God and the angels are watching over you and your family, supporting you in all ways.

∴ 805 ∴

You're being Divinely guided to make some healthy and positive changes, which will help you have a better life in the long run. The sooner you make these changes, the sooner your finances and other parts of your life will heal.

∴ 806 ∴

God is ensuring that your material needs for shelter, food, and such are met. Give any worries about your finances to God, and trust that you're being Divinely helped.

∴ 807 ∴

Because you're listening to and following your Divine guidance, your career and finances are on track. Keep up the good work.

∴ 808 ∴

Everything you need is supplied to you in abundance. Open your arms to receive all of the good that your Creator bestows on you now. This abundance comes to you in many ways, including ideas, opportunities, and people who offer to help you. Be sure to notice and follow these answers to your prayers.

⁙ 809 ⁙

God is supporting your Divine life purpose, ensuring that all of your needs are met as you focus on your spiritual career.

⁙ 810 ⁙

Give any money worries to God, who will lift your faith so that you can attract the highest experiences and the best possible outcomes.

⁙ 811 ⁙

As long as you hold positive thoughts and feelings concerning your finances, all of your bills will be paid and you'll experience steady abundance.

⁙ 812 ⁙

Trust that your prayers, affirmations, and visualizations about your career and finances are working, because they are.

⁑ 813 ⁑

Your prayers and positive thinking have rallied the full support of the ascended masters, who are lifting you and this situation to its highest level and best possible outcome.

⁑ 814 ⁑

The angels ask you to hold positive thoughts about your career and finances so that you can attract the best outcome.

⁑ 815 ⁑

Your new practice of affirmations and visualization is having a beneficial effect on your career and finances.

⁑ 816 ⁑

It's vitally important that you trade any worries about money for affirmations and prayer, to ensure the best possible outcome.

⁂ 817 ⁂

Your ideas and thoughts about your career are right on course, and will bring you a raise or a promotion.

⁂ 818 ⁂

Your positive affirmations about your career and finances are working, so keep going.

⁂ 819 ⁂

As long as you hold positive thoughts about your Divine life purpose, you'll be supported in this endeavor.

⁂ 820 ⁂

Trust that God is watching over you and your family, ensuring that your needs are provided for.

⁂ 821 ⁂

As you stay positive and filled with faith, your financial situation improves rapidly.

⊹ 822 ⊹

The more that you stay optimistic, the better your financial situation gets.

⊹ 823 ⊹

The ascended masters are buoying your faith and optimism about your finances because they know the miraculous power of faith.

⊹ 824 ⊹

Lean upon the angels to stay positive about your financial situation, and borrow their absolute faith that everything is just fine with respect to money.

⊹ 825 ⊹

As you go through changes in your finances and career, your optimism is more important than ever. Keep the faith that all of your financial needs will be met, now and in the future.

⁙ 826 ⁙

Instead of worrying about money, relax and stay positive so that Divinely inspired ideas can show you how to make money in meaningful ways.

⁙ 827 ⁙

Congratulations! You're on the right path, and money is flowing your way!

⁙ 828 ⁙

There's a huge connection between how much faith you have in your financial abundance, and how much financial abundance you experience. Keep the faith, for it is the magical ingredient in your financial life.

⁙ 829 ⁙

You already have, and always will have, enough money to devote yourself to your life purpose, so long as you stay filled with faith and optimism.

✣ 830 ✣

Heaven has heard your prayers for financial assistance and is helping you increase your financial flow. Be sure to notice and follow any intuition that guides you to take positive action, as this is a primary way in which Heaven helps you help yourself.

✣ 831 ✣

The ascended masters are helping you to stay positive with respect to your finances, as they know that positive affirmations are magnetically manifesting your desires.

✣ 832 ✣

Trust that the ascended masters are supporting you in all ways.

✣ 833 ✣

You've been praying to receive financial help, and it's here! You're surrounded by loving and powerful ascended masters who have answered your call for help.

❖ 834 ❖

The angels, archangels, and ascended masters have heard and answered your prayers for help with respect to paying the bills and taking care of your earthly needs.

❖ 835 ❖

The changes that you're making or considering will prove to be answers to your prayers, because these new approaches will bring you vast rewards.

❖ 836 ❖

Give any worries about money to the ascended masters, who are watching over, protecting, and supporting you.

❖ 837 ❖

You're on the right path as you follow your Divine intuition about your career and finances.

⁖ 838 ⁖

Keep prayer and spirituality at the center of your consciousness, and avoid focusing on the material aspects of life (especially money).

⁖ 839 ⁖

The ascended masters say that you'll be able to financially support yourself through your spiritually based career.

⁖ 840 ⁖

God and the angels are watching over you and your loved ones, ensuring that you are all provided for.

⁖ 841 ⁖

Keep a positive outlook, as the angels say that your optimism will attract greater good into your life.

⁖ 842 ⁖

Trust that the angels are blessing and helping you with your career and finances, because they are.

⁘ 843 ⁘

Your prayers for help at work have been heard and answered by the angels and ascended masters.

⁘ 844 ⁘

The archangels and angels are supporting you in all ways, including helping you with financial flow and abundance.

⁘ 845 ⁘

The angels are helping you make positive and healthy changes in your career and finances. You're supported through these changes.

⁘ 846 ⁘

The angels are assisting you with all of your material needs. Lean on the angels more often, and give any worries to them.

⁘ 847 ⁘

The angels say that you're going in the right direction with respect to your career and finances.

⁛ 848 ⁛

You are fully supported in all ways by the angels. Be open to receiving their help, as the more you receive, the more you can share with others.

⁛ 849 ⁛

The angels are reassuring you that you're financially supported as you devote yourself to your spiritually meaningful career path.

⁛ 850 ⁛

The changes that you're making are Divinely inspired and will help you attain new levels of abundance in your life.

⁛ 851 ⁛

Your new and positive thinking style is resulting in an increased flow of money and other areas of abundance.

⁛ 852 ⁛

Trust that you're making the right move with your career and finances, because you are.

853

Your prayers for help with your finances have been heard, and answered by giving you Divine intuition to make some much-needed and healthy life changes. Make these changes and watch the flow of abundance come to you.

854

The angels are helping you heal your career and financial life by guiding you to make positive changes. Be sure to follow your intuition.

855

Huge increases in your financial flow are occurring right now.

856

The financial pressure that you previously felt is lifting, and is being replaced by the experience of financial security and abundance.

⁙ 857 ⁙

You're making the perfect changes at the perfect time, which will enable you to heal your career and finances. Keep going!

⁙ 858 ⁙

To heal your career and finances, you've got to make some positive and healthful changes in your life. You already know what you need to do, so trust this knowledge and act upon it without delay.

⁙ 859 ⁙

To experience more fulfillment, a greater sense of meaning and purpose, and a steady financial flow, change your career focus so that it's more spiritually based.

⁙ 860 ⁙

Give any financial fears to God, who is ensuring that your needs are met.

⁘ 861 ⁘

Instead of worrying about money, pray. Worry attracts problems, while prayer attracts solutions.

⁘ 862 ⁘

Trust that all of your financial and material needs are taken care of, because they are.

⁘ 863 ⁘

The ascended masters have heard and answered your prayers for material and financial support. Give them any cares or worries, and follow their Divine guidance . . . which comes to you as thoughts, feelings, or ideas to take positive action steps.

⁘ 864 ⁘

The angels are watching over you and your loved ones, ensuring that all of your material needs for shelter, food, and such are met.

⁛ 865 ⁛

To overcome financial issues, change your thoughts and actions so that they're totally aligned with your true beliefs. The more authentic you are, the more abundance you experience.

⁛ 866 ⁛

Instead of worrying about money (which never helps anything, and often worsens the situation), turn to spiritual avenues of prayer and meditation (which *always* help).

⁛ 867 ⁛

You're headed in the right direction with your ideas and actions about your career. Move forward confidently, and you'll see and experience the light.

⁛ 868 ⁛

You are experiencing financial security, and the old days of financial stress are now behind you.

⁘ 869 ⁘

As you devote yourself to your spiritually based career, all of your financial needs are taken care of.

⁘ 870 ⁘

You're working in partnership with God's infinite wisdom by praying and then following your inner guidance. As a result, you're experiencing Divine harmony and abundance.

⁘ 871 ⁘

Keep up your positive thoughts, affirmations, and visualizations about abundance, because these practices are having positive effects.

⁘ 872 ⁘

Trust that you're on the right career path, which will ensure that you experience emotional, spiritual, and financial fulfillment.

⁂ 873 ⁂

The ascended masters are assuring you that you have a steady flow of support and abundance for everything that you need.

⁂ 874 ⁂

You're listening to your angels' intuitive guidance, and thus have ensured that every good door is opening for you.

⁂ 875 ⁂

The changes that you're making or considering are healing your career and finances. Move forward with these changes confidently.

⁂ 876 ⁂

You're taking the right steps to make sure that your material and financial needs are met.

⁂ 877 ⁂

You are absolutely on the right path, so keep going. Your present route brings spiritual and material rewards.

⊹ 878 ⊹

Your present path ensures that you are completely supported financially. You have chosen well.

⊹ 879 ⊹

Continue working toward your dreams and desires, as they're the basis of your Divine life mission. Your finances are taken care of as you devote yourself to your purpose.

⊹ 880 ⊹

The Creator is supporting you in all ways. Give any cares or worries, particularly concerning money, to God.

⊹ 881 ⊹

Doors are opening for your career and finances, and you can help with the flow of abundance by practicing daily positive affirmations such as: *I now open my arms to receiving the loving gifts that the Universe brings to me and to everyone.*

⁘ 882 ⁘

As long as you have faith in your heart, your financial situation will continue to flow and improve.

⁘ 883 ⁘

You are receiving Divinely guided help with your career and finances, primarily from the ascended masters (such as Jesus, the saints, Ganesh, and so forth).

⁘ 884 ⁘

The angels have heard your prayers for increased finances, and they're helping you with this issue right now.

⁘ 885 ⁘

There's a positive change coming with respect to your career and finances, such as a raise, promotion, or an unexpected windfall.

⁘ 886 ⁘

The only blocks in your financial flow are worries and fears. Give any cares or concerns to the angels, and you'll experience increased abundance.

❖ 887 ❖

You're on the right path concerning your career and finances. Keep up the good work!

❖ 888 ❖

This is a very auspicious sign of complete financial support from the Universe. Money is flowing in your direction!

❖ 889 ❖

You are financially secure as you devote yourself to working on your spiritual interests and giving of service to others (which is the basis of your Divine life mission).

❖ 890 ❖

God is completely supporting you and your Divine life mission.

❖ 891 ❖

Put your entire focus on answering the question, *How can I serve and make the world a better place?* and all of your material needs will be taken care of.

❖ 892 ❖

Trust that your Divine life mission is supported by the Universe. Give any worries or concerns about money to Heaven.

❖ 893 ❖

You have a close connection with the ascended masters, who are supporting and guiding you along the path of your Divine life purpose.

❖ 894 ❖

Your angels are ensuring that all of your material needs are met while you devote yourself to working on your Divine life mission.

❖ 895 ❖

By making your career more spiritually based, you walk upon the path of your Divine life purpose, and experience the full support that comes from being in your right livelihood.

⁜ 896 ⁜

Instead of worrying about your career or finances, pray and affirm that all is well. Your spiritual career is abundantly supported in all ways.

⁜ 897 ⁜

You're on the right path with respect to your spiritually based career, and all doors are opening for you.

⁜ 898 ⁜

As long as you keep your career focused on serving a meaningful purpose, you are fully supported financially, spiritually, emotionally, and intellectually.

⁜ 899 ⁜

Let go of any tendencies to procrastinate about your spiritual career and Divine mission; and know that the sooner you take guided action, the sooner you'll experience the bliss and abundance that accompanies your purpose.

∴ 900 ∴

This is a strong message from God, urging you to devote your time and energy toward your Divine life purpose, which is much needed in this world. Ask God for guidance as to what your next step should be.

∴ 901 ∴

Stay in steady contact with God concerning your spiritually based career, and follow your Divinely guided intuition with confidence.

∴ 902 ∴

Trust that God is guiding you and your career, because this is true.

∴ 903 ∴

God and the ascended masters are giving you very real guidance about your career path, which you receive as ideas, feelings, and inspiration.

∴ 904 ∴

God and the angels are supporting you as you focus on serving a spiritual purpose in this world.

⁙ 905 ⁙

God is guiding you to make healthful and posi-tive changes in your career so that you can devote your time and energy toward your Divine life purpose.

⁙ 906 ⁙

God is assuring you that all of your material needs will be provided for, as you focus on serving the Divine with your career.

⁙ 907 ⁙

You are accurately hearing and following God's guidance concerning your career.

⁙ 908 ⁙

God is assuring you that you and your spiritually based career are fully supported in all ways.

∴ 909 ∴

Put your entire focus on serving God's loving will through your career. Pray for, and follow, guidance about your career path.

∴ 910 ∴

Continue with your positive affirmations and prayers regarding your purpose in life, because they're working.

∴ 911 ∴

It's very important that you keep a positive mind-set concerning your spiritually based career ideas. Positive thoughts are your most important asset right now.

∴ 912 ∴

Trust that your positive affirmations concerning your career are working, because they are.

∴ 913 ∴

The ascended masters are guiding you to hold positive visions of yourself enjoying your spiritually based career.

⁙ 914 ⁙

The angels are watching over your career, and are guiding you along the path of your Divine life purpose.

⁙ 915 ⁙

The positive changes you've been making are helping your career to blossom into your meaningful mission in life.

⁙ 916 ⁙

As you focus on serving a spiritual purpose through your career, all of your material needs are taken care of.

⁙ 917 ⁙

Your optimism about your career is warranted, as your spiritual focus has put you on the right path.

⁙ 918 ⁙

Your passion about your career ensures your success and support. Follow your heart's guidance.

⋇ 919 ⋇

Devote your entire focus toward serving a spiritual purpose through your career.

⋇ 920 ⋇

Move forward confidently with your career dreams, as God is guiding you safely through this passage.

⋇ 921 ⋇

Trust in your dreams about your spiritually based career, because these ideas are Divinely inspired.

⋇ 922 ⋇

Hold the faith about your Divine mission in life. You are qualified to fulfill this mission, and are supported in all ways. The more you trust and have faith, the better everything goes.

⋇ 923 ⋇

Trust that the ascended masters have heard and answered your prayers about your Divine life purpose.

⁜ 924 ⁜

The angels ask you to "keep the faith" about your spiritually based career, as faith boosts every area of your life.

⁜ 925 ⁜

Instead of worrying about your career, trust that everything is unfolding exactly as it is supposed to, because it is.

⁜ 926 ⁜

Trust that your financial and material needs are being met, as you focus on serving a spiritual purpose through your career.

⁜ 927 ⁜

Your trust and optimism are warranted, because your ideas about your spiritually based career are right on the mark.

⁜ 928 ⁜

Your faith and focus on serving a purpose has put you in the flow of abundant Divine support.

⚜ 929 ⚜

Trust that if you put your entire focus on serving a spiritual purpose through your career, everything else will be taken care of.

⚜ 930 ⚜

God and the ascended masters are working in partnership with you and your career, guiding you along the path of your Divine mission.

⚜ 931 ⚜

The ascended masters are guiding you to hold positive thoughts and emotions concerning your career and purpose in life. Positive thoughts are your greatest career asset.

⚜ 932 ⚜

Trust that the ascended masters are helping your career and Divine life purpose, because they are.

÷ 933 ÷

Your life purpose involves working with the ascended masters to effect positive healings and changes in the world.

÷ 934 ÷

Your Divine mission is guided by ascended masters, angels, and archangels, who work closely with you and your career.

÷ 935 ÷

The ascended masters are guiding you to make healthful and positive changes in your career so that you are completely focused on serving a spiritual purpose through your work.

÷ 936 ÷

All of your material needs are met by the ascended masters, leaving you free to completely focus on serving a spiritual purpose through your career.

⊹ 937 ⊹

You're on the right path of following your Divine guidance about your career and life purpose. Stay in prayerful contact with the ascended masters.

⊹ 938 ⊹

The ascended masters are your partners and co-workers, and they completely support your spiritually focused career.

⊹ 939 ⊹

The ascended masters have heard your prayers about your career, and they've responded that it is important for you to put your entire focus on spiritualizing your work life.

⊹ 940 ⊹

God and the angels are guiding and supporting your Divine life purpose.

⊹ 941 ⊹

The angels ask you to stay positive and optimistic about your mission in life. Know that you are qualified to make a positive difference in this world in a career that's based on your spiritual passions.

⁛ 942 ⁛

Trust that the angels are watching over you and your career, because they are.

⁛ 943 ⁛

The archangels and ascended masters are guiding and supporting your spiritually based career.

⁛ 944 ⁛

Your Divine life purpose involves working with the angels and archangels to help others.

⁛ 945 ⁛

The angels are helping you make positive and healthful life changes so that you're fully on the path of your purpose.

⁜ 946 ⁜

Give any worries or concerns about your career, Divine purpose, or spiritual path to the angels, who are ready to support and guide you in all ways.

⁜ 947 ⁜

The angels say that you're on the right path concerning your spiritually based career.

⁜ 948 ⁜

As you focus your time and energy on serving a spiritual purpose through your career, the angels ensure that all of your financial and material needs are met.

⁜ 949 ⁜

Your Divine life purpose involves working with the angels very closely. Ask the angels for help in building your spiritually based career.

⁜ 950 ⁜

God is helping you change your work life for the better.

⁕ 951 ⁕

Change your thoughts concerning your career so that you see the goodness and love within everyone and everything. Your positive focus helps you get on the path of your Divine life purpose.

⁕ 952 ⁕

Trust that the career changes you're making or considering are a great idea because they bring you in alignment with your Divine life purpose, which means that you feel more fulfilled in all ways.

⁕ 953 ⁕

The ascended masters are guiding you to take action to get your spiritually based career into gear.

⁕ 954 ⁕

You're working closely with the angels to make positive changes in your career so that you can focus on serving your Divine life purpose.

⚜ 955 ⚜

It's time to make the changes that you've been thinking about, especially concerning your career and spiritual focus. These changes are the answers to your prayers.

⚜ 956 ⚜

As you increase the amount of time and energy that you devote to your spiritually based career, your entire life gets better as a result.

⚜ 957 ⚜

The changes that you're making to your career are exactly right, so continue to trust in your ideas and visions.

⚜ 958 ⚜

Now that you're increasing the focus of your career on serving a spiritual purpose, your flow of abundance is also increasing in kind.

⁑ 959 ⁑

It's time to change your career so that it matches your spiritual beliefs, because that's how you find your meaningful mission in life.

⁑ 960 ⁑

Give any worries about your career, spiritual path, or Divine purpose to God, Who holds all of the answers you seek. Listen for the answers through your ideas, feelings, and visions.

⁑ 961 ⁑

The more you hold positive thoughts and feelings about your career and spiritual path, the better everything goes.

⁑ 962 ⁑

Trust that your material needs are being met, as long as you devote yourself to serving a spiritual purpose through your career.

⸭ 963 ⸭

The ascended masters have heard and answered your prayers concerning your career and finances.

⸭ 964 ⸭

Give any cares or concerns about your career or finances to the angels, who await your request for assistance.

⸭ 965 ⸭

Your career and financial situation are improving, as you devote your time and energy toward serving a spiritual purpose through your work.

⸭ 966 ⸭

It's very important that you maintain a loving and spiritualized focus regarding your career. By staying centered in spirituality, you automatically attract everything you want and need.

⸭ 967 ⸭

You're on the right path with your career and spiritual focus, which ensures that all of your material needs will be met.

⸭ 968 ⸭

Instead of worrying about your career or finances, pray. Worry never helps anything, but prayer always improves everything.

⸭ 969 ⸭

Your career will be even more fulfilling and successful when you completely trust in and follow the Divine wisdom and love that is all around and within you.

⸭ 970 ⸭

You're accurately listening to and following God's loving wisdom concerning your career, and as a result, you're on the right path for your Divine life purpose.

⸭ 971 ⸭

Your optimism concerning your career is warranted, because you're taking the right steps for fulfilling an important purpose in this world.

⸭ 972 ⸭

Trust that the spiritual and career path that you're on is the right one for you and your life purpose.

⸭ 973 ⸭

Your prayers about your career and life mission have been heard and answered by the ascended masters, who are guiding and protecting you. Keep listening to your intuition, because these thoughts are actually answered prayers.

⸭ 974 ⸭

The angels are applauding you for following your Divine guidance about your career, as you are now on the path of your life purpose.

⁙ 975 ⁙

The changes that you're making or considering have put you on the right path for your Divine life purpose.

⁙ 976 ⁙

You're on the right path with your career and spiritual focus, which ensures that all of your material needs will be met.

⁙ 977 ⁙

Heaven applauds your devotion toward serving a spiritual purpose in this world.

⁙ 978 ⁙

Continue along your present path concerning your career and spiritual focus, and know that you are being Divinely supported all along the way.

⁙ 979 ⁙

Your decision to completely focus on your spiritually based career is correct.

∴ 980 ∴

God is ensuring that, as you devote your time and energy toward serving a spiritual focus, all of your material and financial needs are met.

∴ 981 ∴

Hold positive thoughts and feelings concerning your career and finances, as your optimism opens important new doors and opportunities.

∴ 982 ∴

Trust that all of your financial and material needs are being met. All you need to do is continue devoting yourself to serving a spiritual focus through your career.

∴ 983 ∴

The ascended masters are assuring you that they are fully supporting you and your Divine life purpose. Trust that all is well, because it is.

∴ 984 ∴

The angels are watching over you and your career path.

⊹ 985 ⊹

The changes that you're making or considering will increase the flow of abundance for your spiritually based career.

⊹ 986 ⊹

All of your material and financial needs are met as you completely focus on serving a spiritual purpose through your career.

⊹ 987 ⊹

You're on the right spiritual, career, and financial path, so keep up the good work!

⊹ 988 ⊹

You've got the Midas touch concerning your career right now, and everything that you do turns to gold. This is a wonderful time to start new ventures, as long as they're completely based on your spiritual guidance and inner truth.

⁙ 989 ⁙

You've attained good balance in your life! You're very spiritually minded, yet have down-to-earth thinking and actions.

⁙ 990 ⁙

God is urging you to completely concentrate on serving a spiritual focus through your career, as an answer to your prayers.

⁙ 991 ⁙

Stay positive and true to yourself in your career choices.

⁙ 992 ⁙

Trust that the career path you've chosen and dreamed about is the right one for your Divine life purpose.

⁙ 993 ⁙

The ascended masters are helping you with every aspect of your spiritually based career, which is the basis of your Divine life purpose.

⁘ 994 ⁘

The angels say that you are teaching about Divine love through your career, which is a much-needed purpose to fulfill.

⁘ 995 ⁘

Keep increasing the amount of time and energy that you devote to your spiritual practice, as your Divine life purpose involves a total focus on spirituality.

⁘ 996 ⁘

All of your material needs are fulfilled as you devote yourself to your spiritually based career.

⁘ 997 ⁘

You're on the right path by focusing upon serving a spiritual purpose that involves teaching the principles of Divine love.

⁘ 998 ⁘

Put your entire focus on serving a purpose in this world that's connected to your natural interests and passions, and all of your financial and other material needs will automatically be taken care of.

∴ 999 ∴

This is a message signifying completion of an important chapter in your life, and now it's time to get to work—without procrastination—on your next life chapter. This number sequence is like an alarm clock, ringing loudly in order to jolt you into working on your life purpose!

ABOUT THE AUTHOR

Doreen Virtue holds B.A., M.A., and Ph.D. degrees in counseling psychology, and is a lifelong clairvoyant who works with the angelic realm. She is the author of the *Healing with the Angels* book and oracle cards; *Archangels & Ascended Masters;* and *Angel Therapy®*, among other works. Her products are available in most languages worldwide.

Doreen has appeared on *Oprah*, CNN, *The View*, and other television and radio programs. She writes regular columns for *Woman's World, New Age Retailer,* and *Spirit & Destiny* magazines. For more information on Doreen and the workshops she presents, please visit **www.AngelTherapy.com**.

You can listen to Doreen's live weekly radio show, and call her for a reading, by visiting **HayHouseRadio.com®**.

NOTES

_____

_____

_____

_____

_____

_____

_____

_____

_____

_____

_____

_____

_____

_____

NOTES

_____

_____

_____

_____

_____

_____

_____

_____

_____

_____

_____

_____

_____

NOTES

_____

_____

_____

_____

_____

_____

_____

_____

_____

_____

_____

_____

NOTES

_____

_____

_____

_____

_____

_____

_____

_____

_____

_____

_____

NOTES

_____

_____

_____

_____

_____

_____

_____

_____

_____

_____

_____

_____

_____

NOTES

_____

_____

_____

_____

_____

_____

_____

_____

_____

_____

_____

_____

_____

YOU CAN HEAL YOUR LIFE, the movie,
starring Louise Hay & Friends (available as
a 1-DVD program and an expanded 2-DVD set)
Watch the trailer at: **www.LouiseHayMovie.com**

THE SHIFT, the movie,
starring Dr. Wayne W. Dyer (available as
a 1-DVD program and an expanded 2-DVD set)
Watch the trailer at: **www.DyerMovie.com**

Colors & Numbers, by Louise Hay

The Divine Matrix, by Gregg Braden

Messages from Spirit, by Colette Baron-Reid

Transforming Fate into Destiny,
by Robert Ohotto

For info on the above or on the
app version of ***Angel Numbers 101***,
please visit Hay House (see next page).

We hope you enjoyed this Hay House book.
If you'd like to receive our online catalog featuring
additional information on Hay House books and
products, or if you'd like to find out more about the
Hay Foundation, please contact:

Hay House, Inc.
P.O. Box 5100
Carlsbad, CA 92018-5100

(760) 431-7695 or (800) 654-5126
(760) 431-6948 (fax) or (800) 650-5115 (fax)
www.hayhouse.com® • www.hayfoundation.org

Published and distributed in Australia by:
Hay House Australia Pty. Ltd., 18/36 Ralph St.,
Alexandria NSW 2015 • *Phone:* 612-9669-4299
Fax: 612-9669-4144 • www.hayhouse.com.au

Published and distributed in the United Kingdom by: Hay
House UK, Ltd., Astley House, 33 Notting Hill Gate,
London W11 3JQ *Phone:* 44-20-3675-2450
Fax: 44-20-3675-2451 • www.hayhouse.co.uk

Published and distributed in the Republic of South Africa by: Hay House SA (Pty), Ltd., P.O. Box 990, Witkoppen 2068 • info@hayhouse.co.za www.hayhouse.co.za

Published in India by: Hay House Publishers India, Muskaan Complex, Plot No. 3, B-2, Vasant Kunj, New Delhi 110 070 • *Phone:* 91-11-4176-1620 *Fax:* 91-11-4176-1630 • www.hayhouse.co.in

Distributed in Canada by: Raincoast Books, 2440 Viking Way, Richmond, B.C. V6V 1N2 *Phone:* 1-800-663-5714 • *Fax:* 1-800-565-3770 www.raincoast.com

Take Your Soul on a Vacation

Visit **www.HealYourLife.com®** to regroup, recharge, and reconnect with your own magnificence. Featuring blogs, mind-body-spirit news, and life-changing wisdom from Louise Hay and friends.

Visit **www.HealYourLife.com** today!